The ENCYCLOPEDIA of UNBELIEVABLE FACTS

chartwell
books

CONTENTS

HELLO FACT-FINDERS!

Let's face facts, **FACTS** are just fascinating, especially the unbelievable ones. They open our eyes, they boggle our brains, and they help us to impress our friends and families. If you're a philomath—that's someone who loves facts—and you want to be a pantomath—that's someone who knows everything—then this is the book for you.

WHAT IS AN ENCYCLOPEDIA?

An encyclopedia is a book that explains how the world works. It's often packed with facts about a variety of subjects, or lots of facts about one particular subject. This encyclopedia is bursting with 500 facts, but they are **UNBELIEVABLE**. Soon, you'll be saying, "No way! That can't be true."

As a matter of fact, in this book there are 10 chapters, which explore different subjects, from animals and the human body to history and space. Each chapter contains 50 questions, and each answer is a fact.

HOW TO READ THIS BOOK

There is no right way to read *The Encyclopedia of Unbelievable Facts*, but here are a few ideas to get you started. Feel free to come up with your own favorite way, too.

1. Where will you start? Will you dive in to your favorite subject and test yourself?
2. Or will you read from page 1 to page 112? Watch out, your brain may grow as you go...
3. You can read by yourself, then impress your pals with your astonishing facts.
4. Or you can read out the questions to friends and family. How many do they get right?
5. If you're feeling tricksy, you can read an answer and ask, "What's the question?"
6. You can look at the pictures first, then read the wow-that's-unbelievable fact.
7. You can read the book on the couch, or under a tree, or in the dark with a flashlight.
8. You can go to the index and look up a topic, then find a mind-boggling fact.
9. You can skip to an unfamiliar subject and learn mind-stretching things.
10. You can read to learn the most amazing new things. Or, of course, just to have fun.

What are your top three facts from each chapter?

What are your top 10 facts from the entire book?

HUMAN BODY

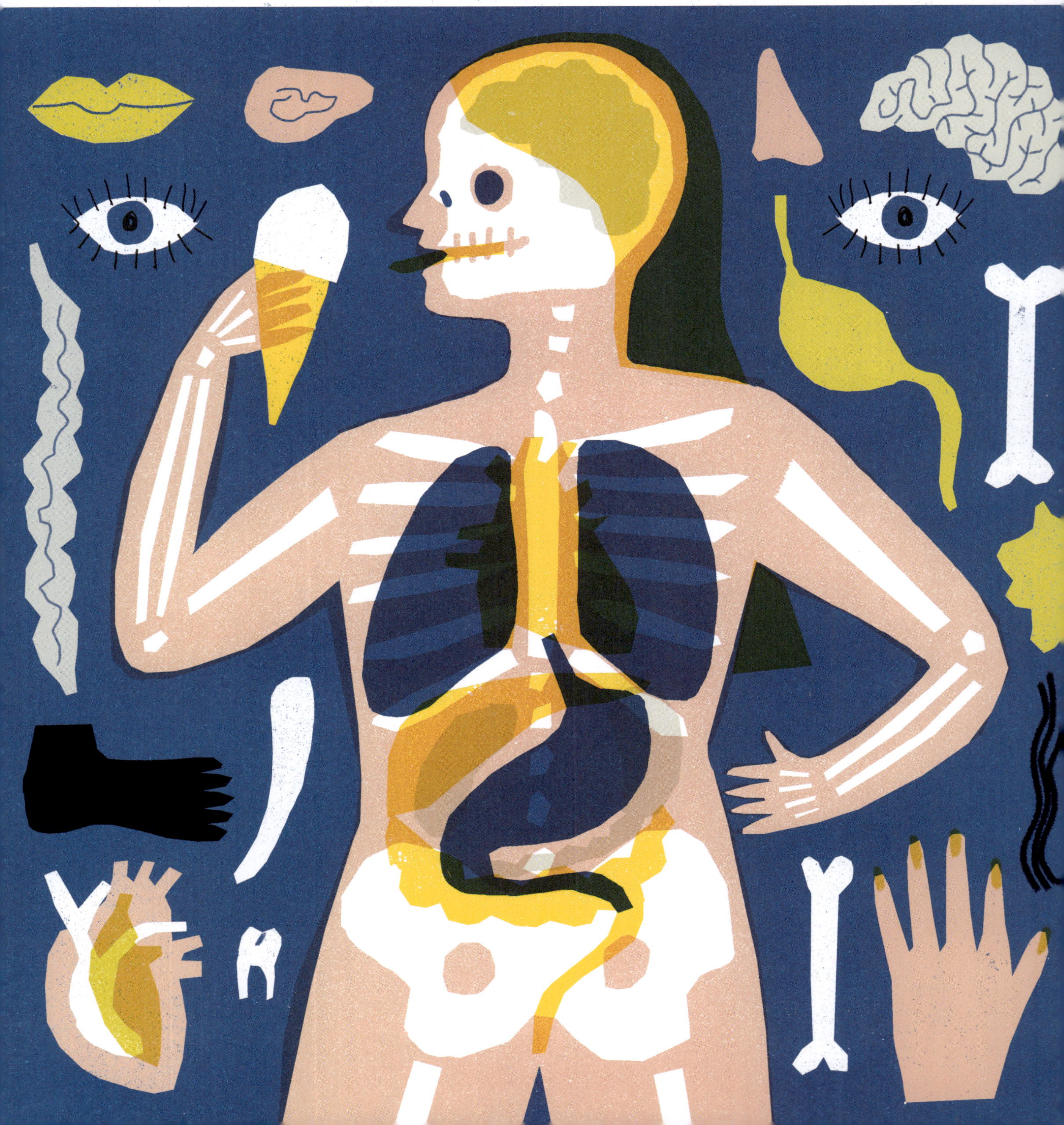

Q There are about 7,000,000,000,000,000,000,000,000,000 (that's 7 octillion) of them in your body. What are they?

A Atoms. Everything in the universe is made from atoms. An atom is a basic unit of matter. This period "." is about 20 million times the size of an atom.

Q How many cells are there in the human body?

A About 37 trillion. All living things are made up of cells.

Q Who has more hairs on their body, a human or a chimp?

A A human has as many hairs as a chimpanzee, but thin human hairs are much harder to spot than a chimp's thick ones. Hair helps us to control our body temperature.

Q What's so special about DNA? And what do the letters stand for?

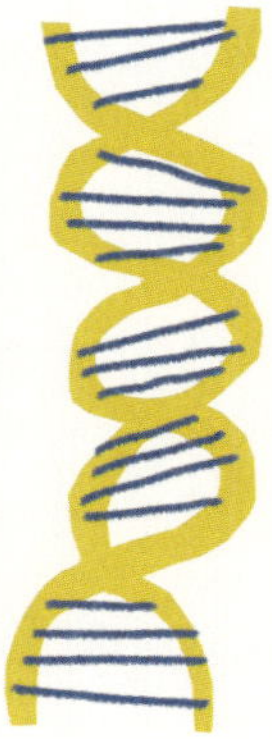

A DNA stands for deoxyribonucleic (de-oxy-rib-o-nu-cle-ic) acid. Try saying it out loud. DNA is found inside cells. It contains the information the body needs to work and grow.

Q How fast do messages travel to and from your brain?

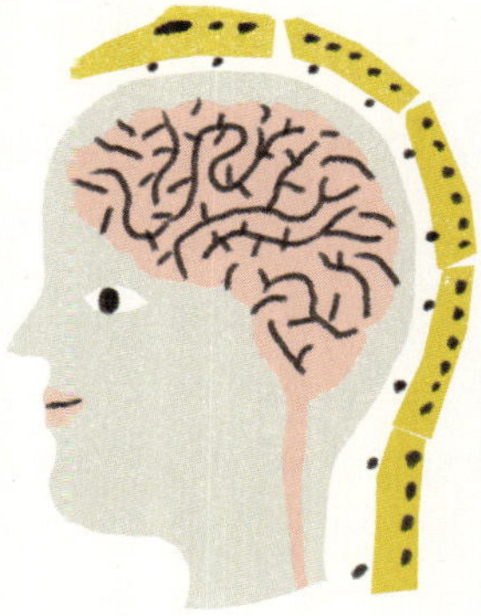

A Nerves send signals, or messages, to and from the brain. The speediest signals can travel as fast as a bullet train.

Q Which sense is the fastest?

A Hearing. Clap your hands to celebrate. Sound travels from your ear to the brain in just 0.05 seconds. That's 10 times faster than a message between your eyes and your brain. It beats touch and smell, too.

Q How many times do you blink in a minute?

A About 20. In total, your eyes are closed for about 90 minutes every day. Blinking keeps your eyes wet so they work properly. Birds blink, too, but only one eye at a time.

Q What lives on eyelashes?

A Microscopic, or extremely tiny, bugs called eyelash mites might live on your lashes. You would need a microscope to see them.

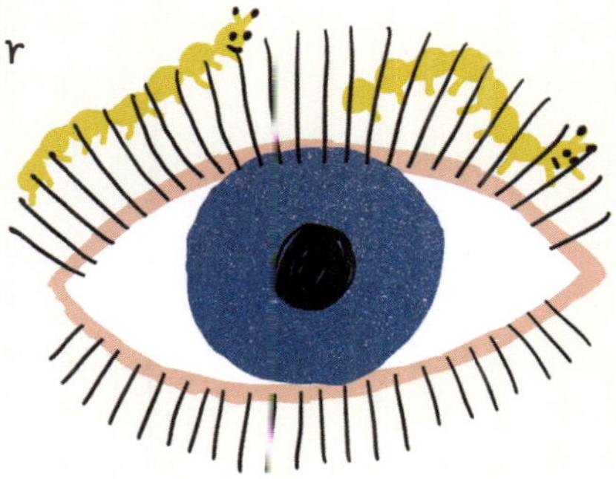

Q How much gunk does your nose make?

A Almost seven teacups of gunk called mucus, or snot, every day. Most of it runs down your throat without you noticing it! The inside of your nose is similar to a doormat that stops dirt and germs from getting inside your body.

Q What happens about 40 million times a year in your body?

A Your heart beats. That's around 70 beats a minute and over 100,000 beats a day. Put your hand to your chest and feel it!

Q Which part INSIDE your body goes red when you're embarrassed?

A Your stomach. When you are embarrassed, your body makes a hormone called adrenaline, which helps more blood flow. The lining of your stomach becomes red. You're blushing on the inside, too!

Q Over a lifetime, what might you spend 92 days doing?

A Going to the bathroom! You'll also spend three and a half years eating. Delicious.

Q How many times does one blood cell travel through the heart each day?

A More than 1,000 times. That's a lot of zip-zapping around the body.

Q How long is the longest recorded bout of hiccups?

A 68 years. There are all kinds of suggested cures for hiccups, including thinking about pineapples and being surprised. What works for you?

Q Which goes fastest—a fart, a sneeze, or a cough?

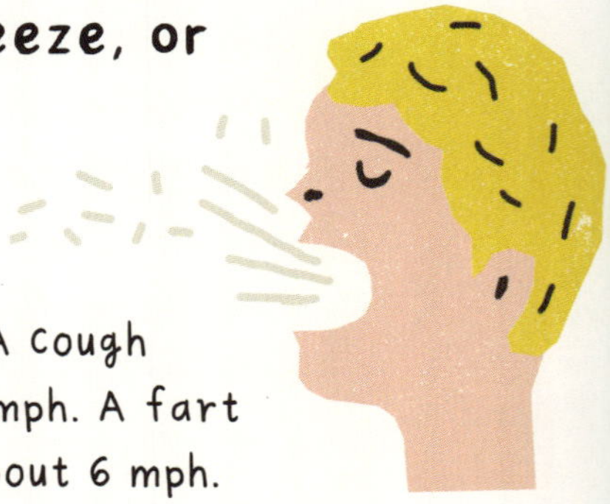

A A sneeze is the winner at about 99 mph. A cough goes at about 50 mph. A fart finishes last at about 6 mph.

Q How many kinds of germs do you have in your belly button?

A Around 67. Germs, called bacteria, are tiny living things. Some bacteria are good and some are bad for the body.

Q Which precious metal can be found in your hair?

A Gold. Your locks are made from a tough protein called keratin. Hair also contains tiny traces of gold. Babies have more gold in their hair than adults. Other parts of your body, including your heart, contain gold, too.

Q Why do only some farts smell?

A Only 1% of farts contain sulfur, which is the chemical that makes them stinky. The other 99% of farts contain gas that doesn't smell. Eating lots of sulfur-rich food, such as beans, makes your farts smelly.

Q What do you do when you eructate?

A Burp. Air from your stomach is released through the mouth—excuse you—to stop the stomach from expanding too much. In many cultures, it's good manners to belch after a delicious meal.

Q And breathe... how many breaths do you take a day?

A Around 20,000 a day, about 600 million over a lifetime. You breathe in oxygen and push out waste gas. As you breathe, most of the air goes in and out of one nostril. Every few hours, the other nostril takes over.

Q Where is the biggest muscle in your body?

A You might be sitting on it right now. It's the *gluteus maximus*, AKA your posterior, tush, bottom, or butt.

Q Can a smile make you happy?

A Yes. Scientists have found that smiling makes your brain release chemicals that make you feel good. Keep smiling!

Q Which part of your body is similar to an octopus tentacle?

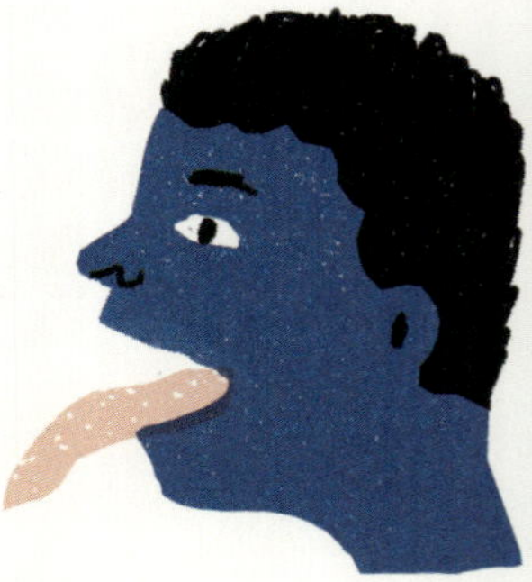

A Your tongue. It can bend, change shape, and stretch just like an octopus tentacle.

Q What's the smelliest thing in the world?

A Tricky. Everyone has their own "nose opinion." But the cheese Époisses de Bourgogne is banned on French public transportation because it is so smelly. And the stinky durian fruit, which smells like drains, is banned from some hotels in Asia.

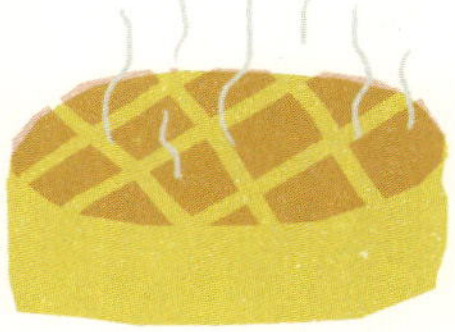

Q Can you tickle yourself?

A No, you can't. There's always an element of surprise with a tickle and you can't surprise yourself. Here's a tip, in a tickling contest, go for the soles of your opponent's feet, which are one of the most ticklish parts of the body.

Q How old were you when your fingerprints developed?

A You had fingerprints before you were born. A baby growing in its mother's womb has a fingerprint at three months. Each person has a unique, or special, fingerprint.

Q What can't your body do?

A Most people can't lick their elbows. Can you? It's just too far to reach. And it's extremely difficult to sneeze with your eyes open.

Q Where in your body is the Island of Reil?

A Deep inside your brain. It is named after the German scientist, Johann Christian Reil, who first described this area of the brain that is connected with emotions, language, and decision making.

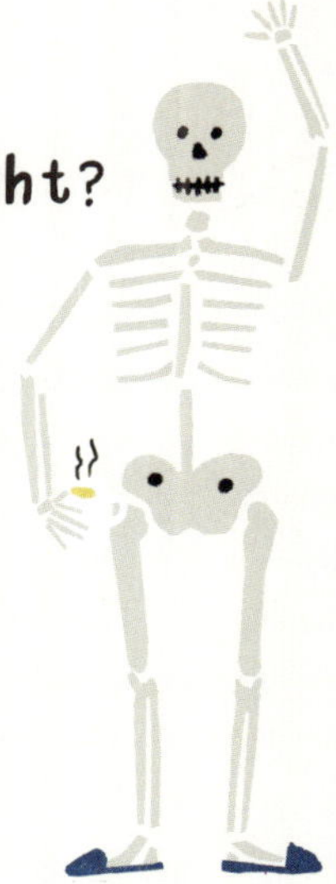

Q Do you grow overnight?

A Yes, you're usually about 8 mm taller in the morning. During the day, when you're upright, soft stuff between your bones, called cartilage, is squished. In bed, the cartilage stretches out so you are slightly taller in the morning.

Q Which has more bones, your hand or your foot?

A Your hand. Each hand has 27 bones and each foot has 26.

Q Take one step. How many muscles have you used?

A Up to 200 muscles.

Q Over a lifetime, how many years might you spend asleep?

A About 33 years, if you live until you're nearly one hundred. Sleep helps the body to repair and makes energy for the next day.

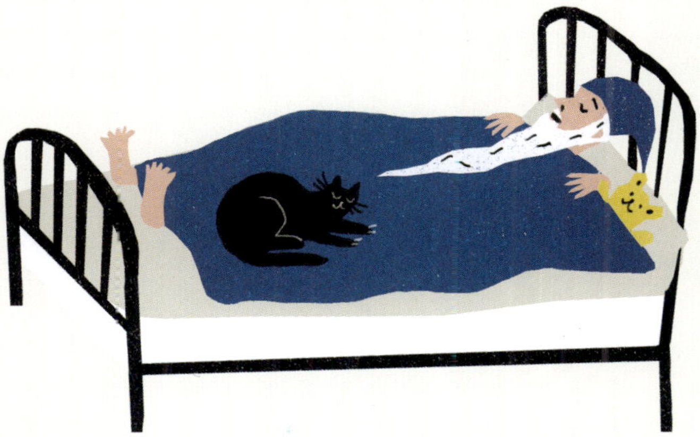

Q What does a flatologist study?

A Farts. Flatulence, or farting, is good for you. Everybody farts to get rid of gases made from chewing and digesting food. A person might fart up to 15 times a day. That's enough gas to fill a balloon. To be clear, that's a party balloon, not a big hot-air balloon. Pop!

Q What's a borborygmus?

A It's the rumbling noise your stomach makes when you're hungry.

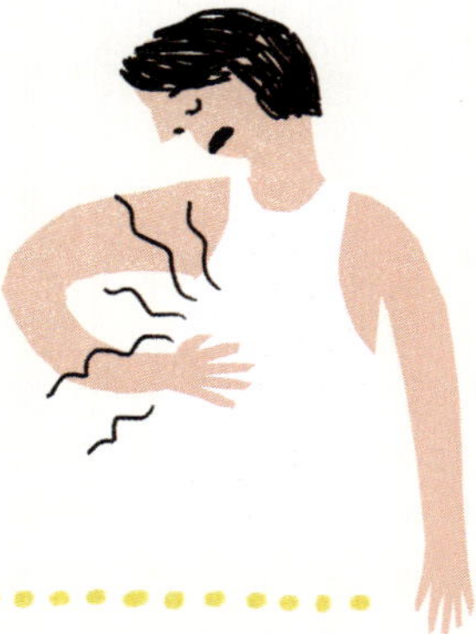

Q Who has more bones in their body, an adult or a child?

A An adult has 206 bones but, mysteriously, a child has more—300 bones. As a child grows up, some bones, including bones in the skull, join together.

Q In the time it takes to read this question, how many babies will have been born in the world?

A Approximately four babies are born every second. Say it takes five seconds to read the question—that's 20 babies!

Q Every minute, you lose 30,000 of what from your body?

A Skin cells. Skin is always replacing itself. New skin cells move up to the surface, then flakes of dead skin fall off.

Q Do hairs and nails continue to grow after death?

A No, this is just a myth made popular by spooky movies with long-haired skeletons. Hair and nails only grow on living people.

Q Imagine your small intestine is one long strand of spaghetti. How long would it be?

A The height of three tall adults. Your small intestine coils around inside your belly. It absorbs the nutrients from food.

Q Can body parts be printed?

A Soon, yes, on 3D printers To help in medical operations, scientists are developing ways of printing body parts, including blood vessels and parts of the ear.

Q Which is the sweatiest part of your body?

A Your feet. Feet can become smelly when sweat mixes with germs, called bacteria, which love the creases and crevices in feet.

Q In medieval times, where would you go with a toothache?

A To the blacksmith, who pulled out people's rotten teeth with big pliers and tongs usually used on animals.

Q What did an ointment of honey, human brains, and animal droppings cure?

A It's debatable if it worked, but in ancient Egypt, priests used this concoction to treat eye problems.

Q Can you "catch" yawning?

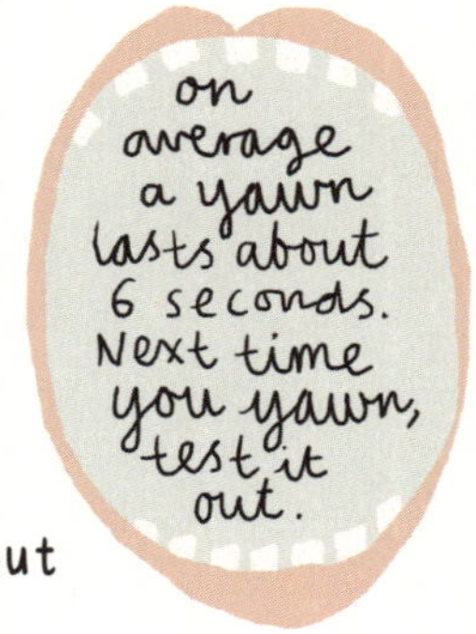

A Scientists are still studying if yawning is contagious or not. Often when one person yawns, people nearby yawn, too, but scientists don't know why.

Q What magic measurements are there in the body?

A The length of your outstretched arms is about the same as your height. You are roughly eight heads high. And try this—is your thumb the length of your nose? It is for most people.

Q Is your body made mostly from solid or liquid?

A Unbelievably, over half of your body is water—up to 60%. And did you know that your brain is 70% water?

Q Over a lifetime, how far around the Earth would you walk—once, twice, or four times?

A About four times.

Q You're lost in the wilderness; can you survive longer without food or water?

A You won't be able to last more than three days or so without water. You could go longer without food, but would feel very weak. Keep your adventures safe.

Q How much power does your brain use?

A This is a light-bulb moment. Your brain uses as much power as a 10-watt light bulb. Also, if you flattened out the wrinkly shape of your brain, it would be about the size of a pillowcase.

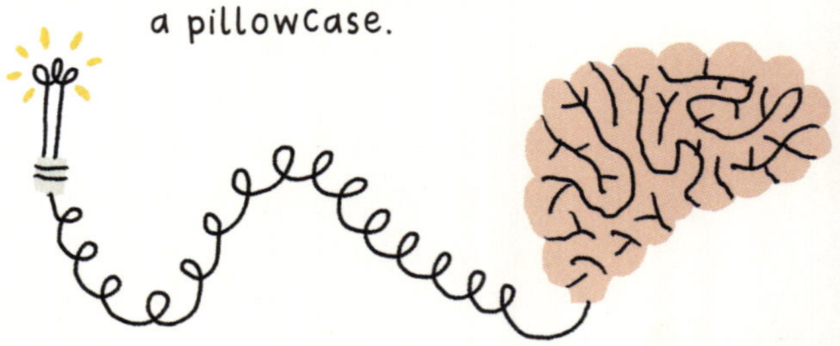

Q **What from inside the body laid end to end would circle the Earth at least twice?**

A Blood vessels that carry blood to and from the heart. Arteries and veins are blood vessels. Think of a blood vessel like a highway that blood cells use to travel around your body.

SCIENCE + TECH

Q What's the biggest machine in the world?

A The Large Hadron Collider, which is built underground in Switzerland. This amazing machine is the size of a small town. It creates similar conditions to the universe at the start of time.

Q Why does a whip make a cracking noise?

A The whip moves faster and faster until—CRACK—it breaks the speed of sound. This is called a sonic boom.

Q Who invented the internet?

A A British engineer called Tim Berners-Lee invented the World Wide Web. This is the part of the internet that contains websites.

Q Who was Dolly the sheep?

A The first cloned sheep. A clone means Dolly was identical in every way to another sheep.

Q What's beard hair got to do with inventing the light bulb?

A In 1878, when American inventor Thomas Edison was working on his version of the light bulb, he tested all kinds of materials for the bulb's filament, or glowing wire. He tried silk, sewing thread, and beard hair.

Q Which British scientist suffered from seasickness?

A Charles Darwin. He spent five queasy years aboard the ship HMS *Beagle*. He traveled the world, studying nature for his book, *On the Origin of Species*, which describes the theory of evolution.

Q What were the first words of the first telephone call?

A "Mr. Watson, come here—I want to see you." The words were spoken in 1876, by Scottish inventor Alexander Graham Bell, to his assistant, Mr. Watson. What would you have said?

Q How fast does the fastest lawnmower go?

A 150 mph. That's over twice as fast as a car can drive on a freeway.

Q Can you un-toast toast or un-cook an egg?

A No. Cooking changes the make-up or structure of the food. It cannot be undone. It's called an irreversible reaction. Alas, burned toast is burned forever.

Q Which animals flew on the first hot-air balloon?

A A sheep, a rooster, and a duck. In 1783, the Montgolfier brothers, who were French inventors, put the animals into the basket of their new invention, called a hot-air balloon. The first flight lasted about eight minutes.

Q Where does oil come from?

A Deep underground, even under the ocean. Oil is made from the remains of ancient marine life such as plants. Over millions of years of pressure and heat, the remains turned into oil.

Q Why is asking questions good for your brain?

A Because it increases the number of connections between your brain cells and keeps your brain active.

Q Can cars be powered by coconuts?

A Yes, and wheat, corn, and even algae from the ocean. Many biofuels come from plant matter. They are an alternative to gasoline, which harms the planet.

Q How did a dish of mold save millions of lives?

A In 1928, Scottish scientist Alexander Fleming noticed on a grubby laboratory dish some mold that killed bacteria, or germs. This mold, called penicillin, is now used as medicine.

Q Why in the world would you give yourself a disease?

A When you are vaccinated, your body takes in dead or weakened germs from a disease. The germs help your body build up a resistance, so you don't get sick.

Q How can you spot a bad egg?

A Put it in a glass of water. As an egg gets older, air enters it and builds up as a gas, which helps it to float. So, if it sinks it's fresh. If it floats—best to avoid!

Q How many riders can the longest bicycle seat?

A 35! The bike is as long as about two buses. The riders pedal together. No wobbling or everyone falls off.

Q Who drew a helicopter-type machine hundreds of years before the helicopter was invented?

A Italian artist Leonardo da Vinci, who painted some of the most famous paintings in the world.

Q What's more powerful, a calculator or the computers that launched Apollo 11?

A When *Apollo 11* launched and landed on the moon in 1969, its computers were less powerful than a calculator we might use today.

Q Is Earth getting lighter?

A Yes. Every year, around 99,208 tons of gas disappears from Earth's atmosphere, into space. But this is a tiny amount in the scheme of things.

Q Where is most of the internet?

A Underwater. There are millions of miles of underwater cables, crisscrossing the oceans. Information, called data, ping-pongs around the world in milliseconds.

Q What's a space elevator?

A This is a new idea scientists are developing. It's a cable that runs from the Earth's surface, way up into outer space. The plan is for space vehicles to climb up and down the cable.

Q How do you open a can without a can opener?

A Curiously, the can was invented almost 50 years before the first can opener. How odd. Before the can opener was invented, you opened a can with a hammer and chisel.

Q How many people use the internet?

A More than 4.5 billion. It's hard to say exactly how many because the number grows all the time.

Q Which famous scientist failed his exams and didn't wear socks?

A German theoretical physicist Albert Einstein. He was a genius and changed the way we understand time and space. He also thought socks were a nuisance.

Q The Wright brothers from the USA invented the first airplane. How did they decide who made the first flight?

A They tossed a coin. Wilbur Wright won, but after take-off, the plane dove quickly. Orville Wright went next and the plane stayed up.

Q How did a pocket of melted chocolate help invent an oven?

A When American engineer Percy Spencer was tracking ships using signals, called microwaves, he noticed the chocolate bar in his pocket melted. Ping! He realized that microwaves could heat food. Soon after, the microwave oven was invented.

Q Who was Johannes Gutenberg and what did he do?

A In about 1440, this German inventor changed the world by inventing the first mechanical printing press. Books no longer needed to be copied by hand. Phew! And ideas could be shared more easily.

Q Which scientist avoided shaking hands with people?

A French biologist Louis Pasteur, because he didn't want to catch a disease. Pasteur discovered how to stop many diseases spreading with heat treatments and vaccines.

Q What's a "BionicOpter?"

A It's a flying robot, based on a dragonfly. It can fly in all directions and hover like a real dragonfly.

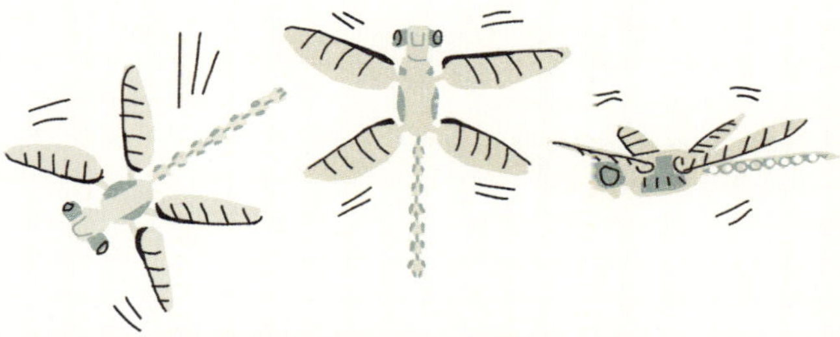

Q How many wheels did the first car have?

A Three. In 1886, German engineer Karl Benz made a three-wheeled "motorwagon." Today many think of it as the first car.

Q What's a "Frankenburger?"

A It's a type of hamburger grown by scientists in a laboratory. Some people call it test-tube meat. It's grown from cells from an animal, such as a cow, but the cow goes on living.

Q What year was the first email sent?

A 1971. Today, nearly 300 billion emails are sent every 24 hours.

Q What's a prokaryote?

A A form of life made of one single cell, such as bacteria. All living things evolved, or developed, from these teeny tiny cells that appeared about 3.8 billion years ago.

Q Who is the only person to win a Nobel Prize in two different sciences?

A Polish chemist Marie Curie. She won Nobel Prizes in chemistry and physics, discovered radium and polonium, uncovered how radiation worked, and helped develop X-ray machines. What a genius!

Q Will a scientist ever invent an invisibility cloak?

A One day, maybe. It's all to do with how light hits an object. Scientists are exploring how to make light appear to travel through an object, so it looks invisible.

Q Which British mathematician was the first computer programmer?

A Ada Lovelace, who lived in the 1800s. She wrote instructions for an early computer, called the Analytical Engine, made by fellow mathematician, Charles Babbage.

Q What's the difference between computer hardware and computer software?

A Computer hardware includes the parts of the computer that you can touch, such as a keyboard and mouse. The software includes the instructions that help you to see and do things on your computer, such as looking things up and playing games.

Q Could women be doctors in ancient times?

A Yes. Many of the earliest known doctors were women. An ancient Egyptian called Peseshet was probably the chief female doctor at the court of the pharaoh, or ruler.

Q What happened before the TV remote control?

A You got up to change the channels on the TV. In the 1920s, when the TV was invented, there were only a few channels and the pictures were in black and white.

Q Who was Katherine Johnson?

A An African American mathematician who helped the USA send humans into space and to the moon. She mapped the route for spacecraft to travel to and from space.

Q Have computers always been machines?

A No. Before electronic computers, teams of people—often women—did the complicated work by hand. They were called "human computers."

Q Which is stronger, gravity or a refrigerator magnet?

A The magnet. Surprisingly gravity, which pulls everything toward the Earth, is less powerful than a magnet.

Q What's the farthest ever flight by a paper plane?

A About 230 feet. That's about the length of a real passenger plane. Can you beat this distance?

Q Did T. rex live closer in time to Stegosaurus or to humans?

A Humans! T. rex and Stegosaurus lived about 85 million years apart. T. rex and humans lived about 65 million years apart.

Q How strong is silk from a spiderweb?

A Superstrong! In fact, it can be bulletproof. The silk is strong because it's light and stretchy.

Q Put these in order of the quietest—rustling leaves, whispering, and breathing.

A Noise is measured in decibels, or db. Breathing is quietest at 10 db. Then rustling leaves at 20 db. Then whispering at 30 db. Shh!

Q How long does it take for a plastic cup to decompose, or break down?

A About 450 years. Scientists say some kinds of plastic might last forever. Remember to reduce, reuse, and recycle.

Q Why do animals become extinct, or die out?

A Species mostly die out because of climate change, loss of habitat, or competition for food. Today, because of human actions, more animals are becoming extinct than at any time in the last 60 million years.

Q Which animal inspired the design of the Japanese bullet trains?

A The kingfisher bird. The shape of its long, streamlined beak was used to make the bullet trains move faster and quieter.

ANIMALS

Q Which animal poops in cubes?

A The wombat. Scientists think the poop is pushed into cube shapes by grooves in its intestine.

Q Which creatures can nap for three years?

A Snails. Also, did you know that a garden snail has about 14,000 teeth?

Q What surprising thing keeps a manatee afloat?

A The power of farting! A manatee is hefty, so to avoid sinking in the water, it has pouches in its intestines, which store farty gases. These gassy pouches help it to float.

Q Is a polar bear white?

A Its skin is black and its fur is actually see-through, not white.

Q Which are the only birds that can fly backward?

A Hummingbirds.

Q Does a hippo make pink milk?

A Nope. But a hippo does release reddish liquids that help to keep its skin moist and to stop sunburn.

Q Which shark can live for over 270 years?

A The Greenland shark. When scientists tested the remains of one of these sharks, they discovered that it had lived for between 272 and 500 years.

Q Which animal poops only once a week?

A The sloth. Its dung is huge, too. One poop can weigh about 2 lbs—that's the same weight as a pineapple.

Q Which animal has the most eyes, a spider or a scallop?

A A spider can have up to 12 eyes. A scallop can have up to 200.

Q What do cows, horses, and giraffes have in common?

A They all sleep standing up.

Q When should you worry if you smell bananas?

A If you're near Africanized honeybees. When these bees are about to attack, they release an alarm scent, which smells like bananas.

Q Which animal brothers and sisters eat each other before they are born?

A Tiger sharks. A pregnant female may have up to 12 pups, or babies, inside her womb. The babies eat each other until only the two strongest pups remain.

Q What can a butterfly do with its feet?

A Taste! It has taste sensors on its feet, which can tell if a plant is tasty or not. A butterfly can also smell things with its antennae, or feelers.

Q What do you call a baby platypus?

A You call it a puggle. Cute! Baby echidnas are also called puggles. Echidnas and platypuses are the only egg-laying mammals in the world.

Q How much poison is there in a pufferfish?

A Enough to kill 30 people. Yikes!

Q How big was the dinosaur *Giganotosaurus'* head?

A The length of a human body. This huge dinosaur was 43 feet long and weighed up to 11 tons—that's five times heavier than a white rhino. It died out 97 million years ago.

Q Who sleeps more—a sloth, a human baby, or a koala?

A A koala, which sleeps up to 22 hours a day. A human baby sleeps up to 16 hours and a sloth sleeps for around 10 hours a day.

Q Why does a dog cock its leg to pee?

A So the pee sprays upward and other animals think the animal that left its scent is taller and bigger and generally more impressive than it really is.

Q How big were beavers in the last ice age?

A About as big as large bears are today.

Q What do dogs, frogs, mice, monkeys, fruit flies, and tortoises have in common?

A They have all been up in space!

Q What kind of "move" is a binky?

A It's a rabbit leap with twisty mid-air kicks. A rabbit does it to say, "I'm happy." Guinea pigs have a similar move, called the popcorn.

Q Which animal has thousands of teeth?

A A slug. As a slug chomps, thousands of tiny teeth on a circular band nibble like a saw.

Q Do unicorns exist?

A Afraid not. This magical beast with its silvery horn is found only in stories.

Q What do you call a group of hyenas?

A A cackle, or a clan. And by the way a group of pug dogs is called a grumble.

Q Is it true that if a cow sits down, it's *going* to rain?

A No, not really. But it is true that some pet dogs can tell if a storm is coming. They sniff and bark more than usual.

Q Which animal eats its own poop for breakfast?

A A capybara. In the morning, its poop is full of nutrients from all the grasses it ate the day before.

Q Which animal almost always gives birth to identical quadruplets?

A The nine-banded armadillo.

Q How many different species are there on Earth?

A Scientists think there are about 8.7 million species.

Q Do any animals live forever?

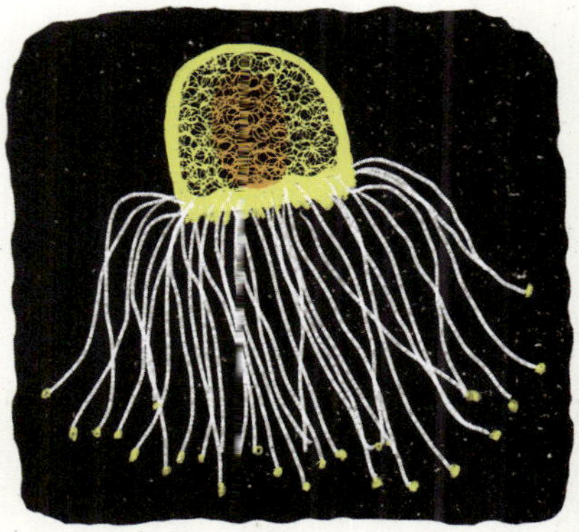

A Yes, the *Turritopsis* jellyfish. This amazing creature does die, but as it decays, a new jellyfish starts to grow. Life just goes on and on.

Q How big is the fart bubble of a blue whale?

A Big enough to fit a horse inside!

Q Who has snowball fights for fun?

A Japanese macaques. Other animals also play games, too. Dolphins have been spotted playing catch with coconuts in the water.

Q What can't an adult elephant do?

A Jump. Its bulky body keeps it grounded.

Q Can any animal daddies give birth?

A Yes. Male seahorses, pipefish, and sea dragons can all give birth.

Q Where is the heart of a shrimp?

A On its head.

Q How do bats sleep?

A Upside down! It's easier for them to take off and fly. They just drop from their perches and flap their wings.

Q What does a bearcat's pee smell like?

A Popcorn! And just so you know, this animal isn't a bear or a cat. It belongs to a family of animals called civets.

Q Which animal has the most legs?

A The *Illacme plenipes* millipede. It has up to 750 legs.

Q What can a kinkajou do with its feet?

A Switch direction to face backward, then run as fast backward as it can forward. A kinkajou can also run down a tree headfirst.

Q What is bufonophobia?

A A fear of toads. FYI, you can't catch warts from a toad.

Q What do these animals have in common—cats, crocodiles, baboons, fish, snakes, and dogs?

A The ancient Egyptians made all of them into mummies.

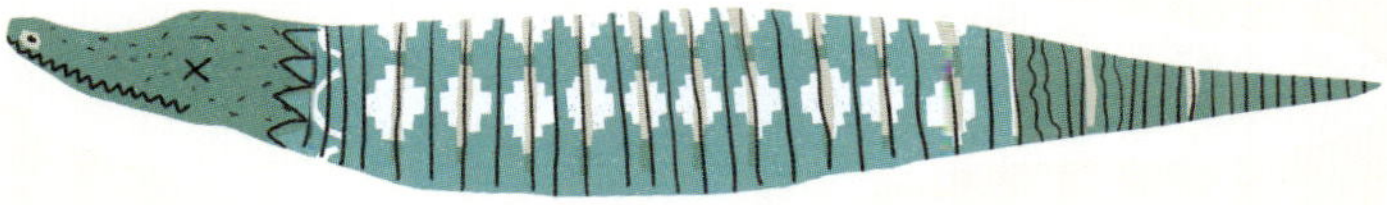

Q How much time does a panda spend eating every day?

A It spends about 16 hours a day chomping and chewing on bamboo.

Q Where did whales live 50 million years ago?

A On land. The fossils, or remains, of the ancestors of whales show they had four legs and lived near rivers.

Q If your tongue were as long as a frog's, how far would it reach?

A To your belly button.

Q Which are the only primates that speak with words?

A Humans. Chimps and gorillas use sounds and signals, but only humans have a complex system of language with words.

Q Which animal group has the most species—mammals, birds, fish, amphibians, reptiles, or invertebrates?

A Invertebrates win. Invertebrates are animals that do not have a backbone, such as snails, worms, and jellyfish.

Q If a cockroach loses its head, what happens?

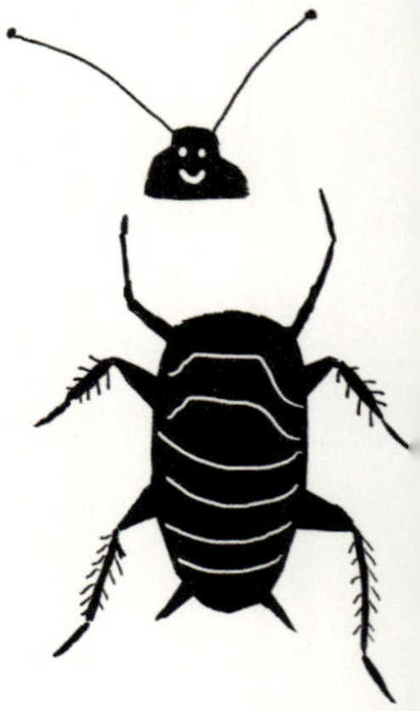

A It can live for over a week—headless. It breathes through its body, where it also has mini-brains.

Q Which color flowers are honeybees attracted to most?

A Yellow, blue, and purple.

Q Why are flamingos pink?

A Because they eat pink algae and shrimp.

Q Which animal is the fastest of all?

A The peregrine falcon. When it dives, it's three times faster than a cheetah.

Q Which animals fall asleep holding hands.

A Sea otters. They hold hands to make sure they don't get separated from their friends.

NATURAL WORLD

Q Where in the world do most volcanoes erupt?

A In the ocean! In an area called the Ring of Fire, in the Pacific Ocean.

Q Which city in the world has the most people?

A Tokyo in Japan. It's a megacity with over 37 million people.

Q What are plankton blooms?

A Huge areas of swirling color in the ocean caused by vast numbers of tiny plants and animals, called plankton. Plankton blooms can be seen all the way from space.

Q How much does an average cloud weigh?

A About 550 tons. That's about the same weight as 80 African bush elephants!

Q How many earthquakes are there every day around the world?

A About 50. Most can't be felt by humans.

Q How much rain forest is cut down every second?

A A patch the size of a soccer field.

Q Which way does water go down the plughole?

A Some think it goes clockwise in the Northern Hemisphere, counterclockwise in the Southern Hemisphere, and straight down at the equator. Many scientists say it can go in any direction, no matter where you are.

Q Exactly how big is a raindrop?

A Weather experts say a raindrop can be between 0.5 mm and 6 mm in diameter.

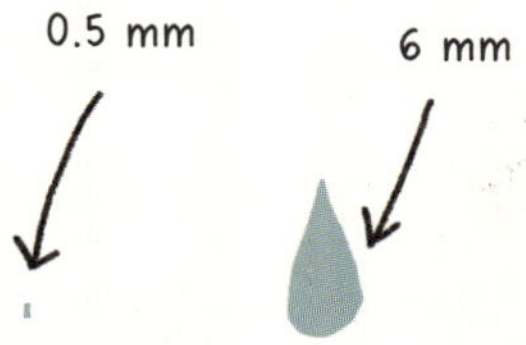

Q What's thundersnow?

A It's when there's thunder and a snowstorm at the same time.

Q How many wooden pencils can an average tree make?

A About 170,000.

Q What's the biggest desert in the world?

A It's not a hot sandy one, it's the icy Antarctic Desert in Antarctica.

Q What does a dendrochronologist do?

A Study the age of trees. They do this by examining tree rings inside a tree trunk.

Q Which island is the biggest in the world?

A Greenland. It's almost 10 times bigger than the UK.

Q Which fruit makes you feel happy?

A Bananas. Scientists say that they contain a natural chemical that makes you feel "up."

Q How fast or slow does a coral reef grow?

A Up to an inch a year—that's roughly the length of a little toe.

Q What is an ice hotel?

A A hotel built out of ice. These hotels can be found in lots of freezing-cold countries like Sweden and Finland. Brrrrr!

Q Who uses a hot-air balloon to go to work?

A Rain forest experts and researchers. They fly above the trees and observe and gather information from below.

Q Why is the Dead Sea called the Dead Sea?

A Because no large plants or animals can live in the extremely salty water. But all the salt does help swimmers to float on top of the water.

Q How old is the rainwater that falls from the sky?

A Even older than the dinosaurs! On Earth, water is recycled again and again in the water cycle.

Q What did some ancient peoples believe diamonds were?

A Splinters from falling stars.

Q Which have been on the planet longer, sharks or trees?

A Sharks. They have been around for 450 million years, while trees have been around for nearly 400 million years.

Q What is brontophobia?

A The fear of thunder and lightning.

Q True or false, there's a tree that's taller than the Statue of Liberty?

A True. A redwood tree growing in California is about 377 feet tall. The statue of liberty is only 305 feet tall.

Q What's a moonbow?

A A moonbow happens when a rainbow is made from the light of the moon. It's rare.

Q Is the Earth covered mostly by water or land?

A 70% of our world is covered by water.

Q Which seed is the largest in the world?

A The coco de mer seed. One seed can be as heavy as a five-year-old child.

Q A rain forest tree can grow as high as which floor of a skyscraper?

A The 20th floor. A rain forest tree can grow to around 295 feet tall.

Q What color is snow?

A It's not white! It's colorless. It reflects all colors, which makes it look white.

Q How hot is the energy from a crackle of lightning?

A It can be up to 60,000 degrees Fahrenheit. That's about five times hotter than the Sun's surface. Ouch!

Q What plant doubles up as a toilet for animals?

A The Low's pitcher plant. Birds eat its nectar then perch their bottoms over a bell-shaped flower and poop. The plant uses the poop to grow. Everyone is happy!

Q Can you fry an egg on a hot sidewalk?

A People try, but many scientists argue it's impossible. The sidewalk would have to be scorching hot for a very long time.

Q What's banned in Antarctica?

A Dogs, because they can carry diseases and infect wildlife.

Q How big is the Pacific Ocean?

A It's massive! It takes up more than 30% of the Earth's surface.

Q Can fish fall like rain from the sky?

A Yes, but it doesn't happen often. When a column of spinning wind, called a waterspout, whirls over the ocean or a lake, it sucks up fish from the water into a cloud. The cloud moves across the sky, then drops the fish to the ground in a different place. It can happen with frogs and snakes, too.

Q Which plant comes into bloom only once a century?

A The towering Queen of the Andes. It blooms every 80–100 years. That's a long wait!

Q Where in the world doesn't it rain?

A Some places in the Atacama Desert, Chile, have not had any rain in more than 50 years.

Q How many of Earth's animals live in rain forests?

A About half of the world's animal species live in rain forests.

Q What will happen to the Sun in roughly 5 billion years?

A Scientists say it will run out of fuel, or energy. It will grow into a giant red star that swallows up nearby planets.

Q How many lightning flashes are happening around the world right now?

A Every second, there are around 40 to 50 flashes of lightning. That's close to 1.4 billion flashes every year.

Q Why was 1816 known as the "year without a summer?"

A The volcano Mount Tambora, Indonesia, blew its top the year before. This caused large dust clouds to block out the Sun and temperatures to fall across the world.

Q What is a growler?

A It's a chunk of ice, about the size of a grand piano. As it melts, trapped air escapes and makes a funny growling sound.

Q What's the world's longest river?

A The River Nile in East Africa.

Q How many seasons are there in Antarctica?

A Two. Summer and winter.

Q Which are the hottest and coldest places on Earth?

A The Lut Desert, Iran, is the hottest. Antarctica is the coldest.

Q Which is faster, a tornado or a hurricane?

A A tornado.

Q Have carrots always been orange?

A For thousands of years, carrots were purple, yellow, and white. It's only in about the last 400 years that they have been grown to be orange.

Q How fast does Earth spin?

A Earth spins at about 1,000 mph. That's as fast as traveling from the North Pole to the South Pole in less than one hour.

Q How many grains of sand are there in the Sahara Desert?

A It's thought there might be around 1,504,000,000,000,000,000,000,000—that's 1.5 septillion—grains. Can you imagine counting each one?

Q Which fruits have their seeds on the outside?

A Strawberries, raspberries, and blackberries.

Q Do trees talk to each other?

A Scientists believe that some trees can warn each other of dangers. When giraffes eat too many leaves from an acacia tree, the tree pumps out a gas that other nearby acacia trees recognize. Then these trees make their leaves taste unpleasant to the giraffes.

SPACE

Q What is a galaxy?

A A huge collection of planets, dust, gas, and billions of stars. Our galaxy is called the Milky Way.

Q How often would you have a birthday on Venus?

A Every day! Venus has the longest day of all the planets. In fact, a day on Venus is longer than a year. If you were born on Venus, it would be your birthday every day.

Q How many Earths would fit inside the Sun?

A Over 1 million.

Q What is the International Space Station (ISS)?

A It's a large spacecraft that orbits the Earth. Astronauts from around the world live and work there when they go into space.

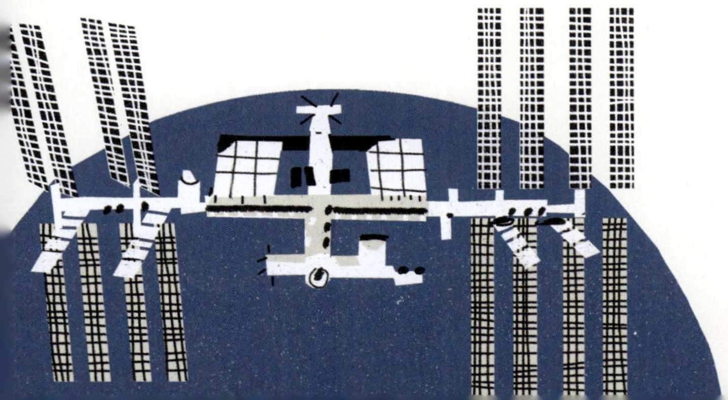

Q Which planet has a blue sunset?

A Mars. The Martian sky usually looks red, but at sunset, fine dust near the Sun makes the sky look blue.

Q What exactly is a light-year?

A It's the distance that light travels in one Earth year. One light-year is about 6 trillion miles.

Q On which planets would your feet not touch the ground?

A Jupiter, Saturn, Uranus, and Neptune, which don't have a solid surface. These planets are called gas giants. They are made up mostly of gases, such as hydrogen and helium.

Q What do astronauts do with their dirty laundry?

A There isn't a washing machine on the ISS, so dirty laundry is loaded into disposable spacecrafts and sent into the Earth's atmosphere, where it burns up!

Q What's the difference between the world and the universe?

A The "world" refers to Earth. The "universe" refers to EVERYTHING, all the planets, moons, stars, galaxies...

Q Is it dangerous to fart in space?

A A fart releases a gas, called methane, which catches fire easily, but so far this hasn't been a problem. The real problem is that the smell hangs around for longer!

Q How many stars are there in the Milky Way?

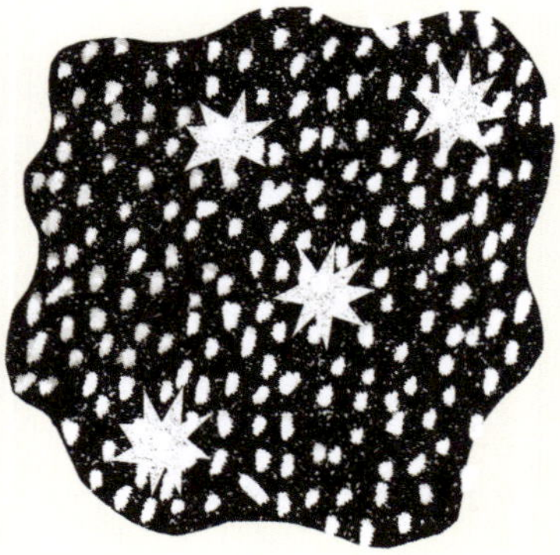

A Scientists say there could be between 100–400 billion stars in our galaxy.

Q What special delivery did the ISS receive in 2001?

A A 6-inch salami pizza. It was the first pizza to be delivered to space!

Q What does space smell like?

A Astronauts say it smells like barbecued meat or burning metal.

Q How long does it take for light from the Sun to reach Earth?

A About eight minutes and 20 seconds.

Q What happens to an astronaut's pee?

A It's recycled. Usually, an astronaut ends up using his or her own clean filtered pee as drinking water.

Q How old is the universe?

A About 13.7 billion years old.

Q What is the solar system?

A Our solar system is made up of the Sun and everything that goes around it. This includes our neighborhood of eight planets, as well as dwarf planets such as Pluto, moons, comets, asteroids, and other small objects.

Q Which way round do the planets spin?

A Most of the planets spin counterclockwise. Venus spins clockwise. So does Uranus, but it's tilted almost on its side.

Q Do your ears pop in space like they do on an airplane?

A No. On a modern spacecraft, the pressure is kept constant. On a plane, the pressure changes, which makes your ears pop.

Q How long does it take for a rocket to reach space from Earth?

A Under 10 minutes.

Q What is the farthest object in our solar system?

A A dwarf planet called Farout, which was discovered in 2018. It is so far away that it takes 1,000 years to orbit, or travel around, the Sun.

Q What's Sagittarius A?

A It's a black hole in the middle of our galaxy. A black hole pulls everything toward it with the force of its own gravity.

Q What happens to an astronaut's poop?

A It's shot out of the ISS and it burns up in space. Bye!

Q What is a Goldilocks Zone?

A The area around a star, where the conditions are just right for life to exist—not too hot and not too cold, like the porridge in the story of Goldilocks.

Q Which planet has storm clouds as big as planet Earth?

A Neptune. This planet has the most extraordinary weather. There are mega-storms and fierce winds.

Q Who flew into space without telling his family?

A Russian astronaut Yuri Gagarin. He was the first human to fly into space. He didn't want his wife to worry, so he didn't tell her the time of his flight.

Q Which neighboring galaxy should we be worried about?

A The Andromeda galaxy. In a few billion years, our galaxy, the Milky Way, and Andromeda, are likely to collide. Crash!

Q Say you're floating in space and you shout at the top of your lungs, do you make a sound?

A Nope! Space is completely silent. Air carries sound waves, but there's no air in space. When astronauts leave their spacecraft, they use radios to talk.

Q Why can't astronauts sprinkle salt and pepper on their food in space?

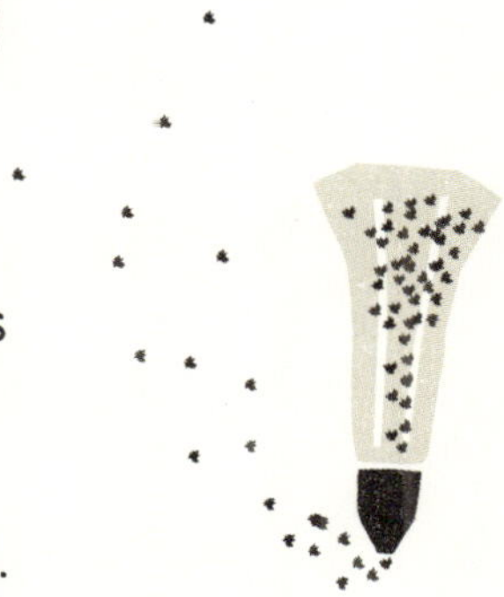

A Because the grains would just float away. Astronauts use liquid salt and pepper instead.

Q What sport did an astronaut play on the moon?

A Golf. In 1971, the American astronaut Alan Shepard was the first person to hit a golf ball on the moon.

Q How did the universe come to exist?

A Scientists believe the universe was made after a massive heat explosion. This idea is called the "Big Bang Theory."

Q Which planet has the shortest day?

A Jupiter. One day is about 10 hours.

Q What do astronauts have to do before going to sleep?

A Buckle up! They attach their sleeping bags to their bunks to stop them from floating away and bumping into things while they sleep.

Q What is a Vomit Comet?

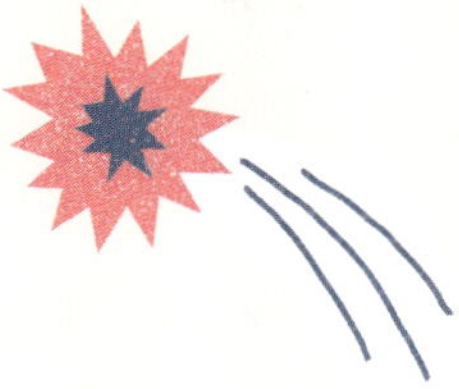

A A training airplane that helps astronauts to cope with feeling weightless in space. It can make some people feel very queasy.

Q Which of these things can be seen from space—the Pyramids of Giza, the Grand Canyon, or the Amazon river?

A Trick question—you can see all three!

Q Can you lift heavier weights in space than you can on Earth?

A Yes. On Earth, a force called gravity pulls everything downward. In space, there's much less gravity, so things weigh less.

Q What is the Sun made of?

A The Sun is a massive ball of scorching hot gases.

Q Are there volcanoes in space?

A Yes. The biggest is found on Mars. It's called Olympus Mons and it's more than twice as tall as Mount Everest.

Q What happens to footprints left on the Moon?

A Nothing. There is no wind or water on the moon, so footprints from the first astronauts who walked on the moon are still there today!

Q How long is a spacewalk?

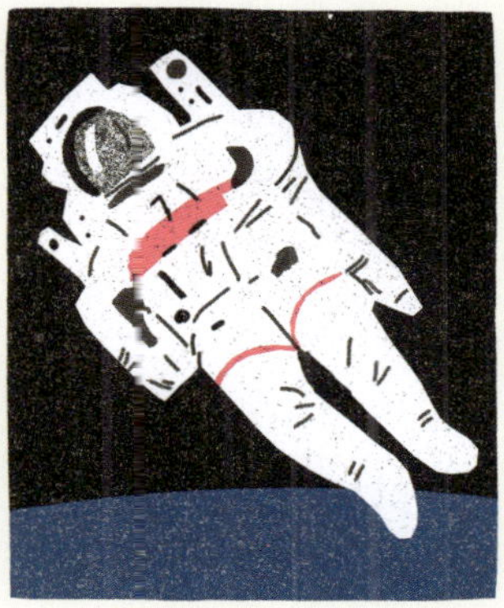

A A spacewalk is when an astronaut leaves a spacecraft and walks in space. It can last for up to eight hours.

Q Where does space start?

A The Kármán Line is a made-up line that helps scientists agree where space officially starts. It's about 62 miles above the Earth.

Q Who was Valentina Tereshkova?

A She was a Russian astronaut, and the first woman in space.

Q Are there diamonds in the sky?

A Yes! In fact, scientists believe the planet 55 Cancri e, which is found in a different solar system from ours, might have a surface made from diamonds.

Q Which Italian astronomer got into trouble for his ideas about space?

A Galileo Galilei. In 1633, he was put under house arrest when he argued that the planets all traveled around the Sun. Today, we know he was right!

Q Why are all spacesuits white?

A Because white reflects heat, keeping the astronauts inside cool.

Q Where would you find the Sea of Clouds?

A On the moon. It's not a sea or clouds though. It's three-billion-year-old solidified lava, which is the hardened rock from a volcano.

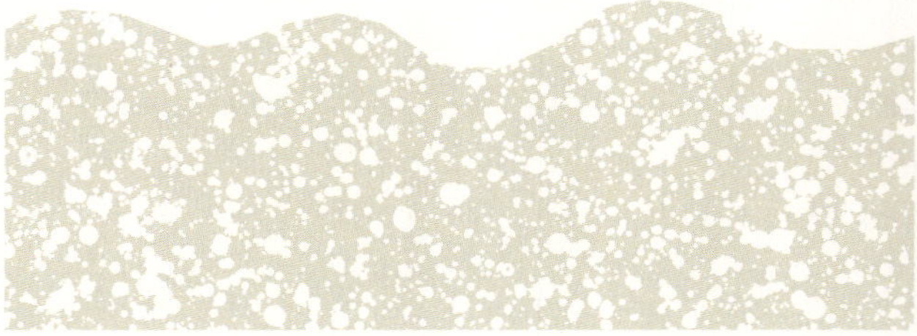

Q How long does it take to fly to Saturn?

A Spacecraft from Earth take between three and seven years to reach Saturn, which is about 746 million miles away.

Q How many sunrises and sunsets does an astronaut see a day from the ISS?

A The ISS orbits the Earth every 90 minutes. That's 16 sunrises and 16 sunsets every day.

Q How do you scratch your nose in a space helmet?

A There's a special patch designed to scratch an itchy nose!

Q Who were Belka and Strelka?

A Two dogs who were among the first animals to be sent into space and come back alive. On August 19th, 1960, the pair spent a day in space before they were safely returned to Earth.

MINDBENDING STUFF

Q What's a googolplex?

A It's an unimaginably huge number made by multiplying 10 by itself again and again. It's so massive it's impossible to write down.

Q What happens to your brain just before you solve a problem?

A Scientists say it "blinks." It briefly shuts down the visual part of the brain so you can focus more. It's like when you shut your eyes so you can think hard, then—ah ha!—you've got the answer.

Q What do the opposite sides of a dice always add up to?

A Seven. Try it and see.

Q What's the world's favorite color?

A Surveys say it's a bluey-green color. What's your favorite color?

Q Who invented zero?

A In 628, an Indian astronomer called Brahmagupta was the first to come up with a symbol called "shunya," which meant empty. This symbol opened up the study of math to all kinds of new possibilities.

Q What is a cubit?

A An ancient unit of measure based on the length of the arm from the elbow to the tip of the middle finger.

Q Is there another "you" in the world?

A No, you're super-special a one-off. But there might be a doppelgänger, who is someone who looks exactly like you.

Q What are the colors of the rainbow in order from top to bottom?

A Red, orange, yellow, green, blue, indigo, and violet.

Q Why was August 8th, 2008, so special?

A In China, the number eight is lucky, so the date 8/8/08 was seen as extra lucky. Thousands of couples married, many with eight bridesmaids and delicious eight-course banquets.

Q If someone asked you to spare a zeptosecond, how long would that be?

A A trillionth of a billionth of a second.

Q What and where is the inferior temporal gyrus?

A It's the part of your brain that remembers numbers and it's behind your ears.

Q Riddle us this: what is as big as an elephant but weighs nothing?

A An elephant's shadow!

Q What's a mathlete?

A An athlete of mathematics, who competes in math competitions and figures out math problems really quickly, without a calculator or pen and paper.

Q Is time travel possible?

A In the movies, yes. In real life, we don't know. Scientists are working on an idea called a wormhole, where space and time might fold together so people can travel through time.

Q What is the Bermuda Triangle?

A It's a part of the Atlantic Ocean, where some people believe planes and ships mysteriously disappear. Other people think there are logical reasons behind the disappearances such as bad weather or human error.

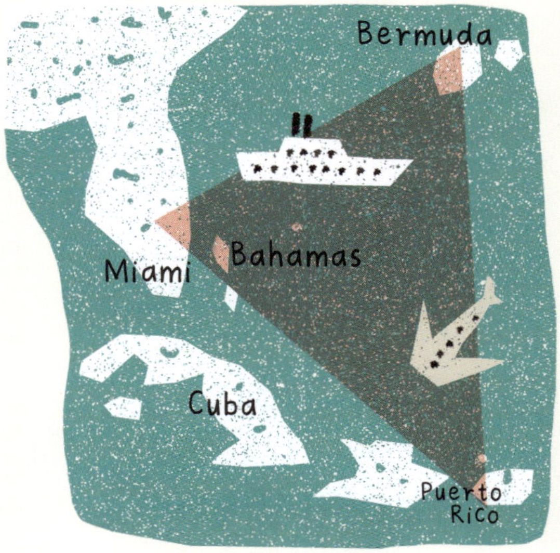

Q How much of the ocean have we explored?

A Only 5%! About 95% remains unexplored.

Q Why are white flags used to surrender?

A In the past, it was probably easier to find white fabric, such as a handkerchief. Also, white wouldn't be confused with an army's colorful banners.

Q What did the Incas do to help them keep count?

A They tied different sized knots onto lengths of different colored string on a device called a "quipu." The knots and colors stood for different numbers. It helped the Incas to count.

Q Which color makes you hungry?

A Scientists think red and yellow make you hungry. That's why lots of food is sold in red and yellow packaging.

Q How many zeros are there in one millinillion?

A A whopping 3,003 zeros.

Q What's a polygon?

A It's a flat, or two-dimensional, shape made from at least three straight lines, such as a triangle or rectangle.

Q Why are some submarines yellow?

A Because yellow can be seen deep under water, making the submarines easier for other ships to spot. Usually research scientists' submarines are yellow.

Q What's spaghettification?

A It's when the force of gravity from a black hole is so strong it stretches and pulls an object into super-long, noodle shapes.

Q What is triskaidekaphobia?

A A fear of the number 13. Around the world many people believe 13 to be an unlucky number, except for in China where it's considered to bring good luck.

Q What color is the blood of an octopus?

A Blue. Its blood contains copper. A human's blood is red because it contains iron.

Q When you're frightened, why do your eyes boggle?

A Scientists say our eyes open wide and our pupils grow bigger when we're afraid so that we can see more clearly what's going on. This also happens when we're surprised.

Q Which ghost gallops around looking for his head?

A The headless horseman. Since medieval times, there have been stories about this ghost tormenting people in search of his missing head.

Q What number does putting your hands on your head mean?

A In medieval times, it meant 1 million. Nowadays, people might think you're just stretching your arms!

Q Brainteaser time: what travels the world, but is always stuck in a corner?

A A postage stamp on a letter.

Q Which is bigger, one trillion or one octillion?

A One octillion. One trillion has 12 zeros and one octillion has 27 zeros.

Q Which soccer players are more likely to score?

A Statisticians, who study numbers, say players who sprint faster and longer have a higher chance of scoring.

Q What color did Queen Elizabeth I of England ban?

A Purple. Only Elizabeth and members of her family were allowed to wear purple. It was banned for everyone else.

Q How did ancient Egyptians tell the time?

A They invented a sundial with a stone pillar that cast shadows to show how time passed over the day. The ancient Egyptians were also the first to split the day into 24 hours.

Q How do you measure the height of a horse?

A In hands. In the past, farmers put their hands one on top of the other to measure the height of a horse for sale. Today, one hand is about 4 inches.

Q How many colors can you see?

A Everybody is different, but on average a person can see about 10 million colors.

Q How many minutes are there in one year?

A 525,600. 527,040 in a leap year.

Q Do we know the answers to all math problems?

A No, there are still lots of big math mysteries. These include the six Millennium Prize Problems—a 1 million dollar prize awaits anyone who manages to solve one!

Q How many peanuts are there in a jar of peanut butter?

A About 540 peanuts. And by the way, there's no butter in peanut butter. It's mushed-up peanuts with a few other ingredients, including sugar and salt.

Q What's the longest amount of time?

A A supereon is an impossible-to-measure amount of time without end.

Q Which century are we in?

A It depends which calendar you use. Most of the world uses the Gregorian calendar, where it's the 21st century. In the Chinese calendar, it's the 48th century.

Q In a room of 23 people, how many might have the same birthday?

A There's a 50% chance two of them will have the same birthday. Hip-hip-hooray!

Q Which seven letters make up all Roman numerals?

A I, V, X, L, C, D, and M.

Q What goes on and on and never ends...?

A Infinity. In mathematics it's shown by this symbol ∞ because the shape of the symbol just goes on and on and on...

Q How did people wake up before the alarm clock?

A In the 1800s in the UK, a person called a knocker-upper would be paid to tap loudly on a customer's bedroom window to wake them. These walking alarm clocks used long sticks or sometimes pea shooters. Rise and shine!

Q Why is the number nine mathematically magic?

A First multiply a number by nine. Then add together the numbers in the answer and it always makes nine. See for yourself: 2 x 9 = 18 then 1 + 8 = 9.

Q What happens when a bull sees red?

A The same as when it sees any other color. It's a myth that if you show a bull a red flag it becomes angry.

Q How many seconds in a lifetime?

A If you live until you are 99, you will live for 3,122,064,000 seconds.

Q Is it possible to see the past?

A Yes—when you look up into space. Light takes such a long time to travel the vast distances across space, that the starlight we see is old—we are looking at the time when the light started traveling and not the light as it is right now.

Q Puzzle time! What gets wet when drying?

A A towel.

Q What happened onboard the Mary Celeste?

A Nobody knows. In 1872, the ship was found floating off-course with plenty of food and supplies, but the captain and crew had disappeared.

HISTORY

Q Exactly when does history begin?

A It's tricky... The universe was formed about 13.7 billion years ago. Life on Earth began about 3.8 billion years ago. And humans evolved between 300,000 and 200,000 years ago.

Q What might you eat at a Roman dinner party?

A Roman dishes included flamingo tongues, roast peacock, and dormice covered in honey and poppy seeds. Wealthy Romans lay on beds and ate with their right hands.

Q What was the Black Death?

A A deadly plague that swept across Asia and Europe in the 1300s. It killed millions of people. It was spread by infected rat fleas.

Q Who was Alan Turing?

A A British mathematician. During World War Two, he helped beat the Nazis by breaking secret codes.

Q How were the first Olympic Games different from our Games today?

A All the competitors were naked! The games were held in Athens, Greece, to honor the god, Zeus. Contests included running and chariot racing.

Q Which king had the shortest reign of all time?

A Louis Antoine of France. In 1830, he reigned for just 20 minutes before he decided it wasn't for him.

Q What did the first American president George Washington use hippo tusks for?

A His teeth! They were used to make his dentures.

Q What did ancient Egyptians do in their spare time?

A They played board games! One popular game was called senet. Some Egyptians were even buried with senet boards.

Q How did the "first" ancient Greek doctor diagnose his patients?

A Today, Hippocrates is known as the "father of medicine." To help find out what was wrong with his patients, he tasted their pee, earwax, and boogers.

Q How did the pirate Blackbeard make himself look devilishly fierce?

A Fire! Blackbeard put flaming matches under his hat and lit candles in his beard. This helped to create his hellish and scary image.

Q How heavy was a medieval knight's full set of armor?

A About as heavy as a seven-year-old child. If the knight fell over, it was a struggle to get up.

Q What did British soldiers do to their boots during WWI?

A Pee in them! The boots were made of tough leather that often gave soldiers blisters, so to soften the insides they would soak them in pee overnight.

Q How did a twisty staircase keep a medieval castle safe?

A A castle staircase was built in a tight spiral with uneven steps. As attackers ran up the stairs, they had little room to swing their swords. Many fell on the steps, too.

Q Which ancient ruler was very fond of hot chocolate?

A The Aztec emperor Montezuma II. It's said he drank up to 50 cups a day.

Q Who ran the first marathon?

A Legend says an ancient Greek messenger ran all the way from the town of Marathon to the city of Athens to deliver news of a military victory. The distance of about 26 miles is the length of the running race today.

Q Who was the richest man of all time?

A Mansa Musa, who was a 14th century West African king. His empire owned almost half of the world's gold.

Q Who got on a bus, sat down, and changed history?

A African American civil rights activist Rosa Parks. On December 1st, 1955, she broke the law by refusing to give up her seat for a white passenger. This sparked protests of support. Eventually, the law was changed.

Q How many languages could Cleopatra, the last ruler of ancient Egypt, speak?

A Experts believe between 7 and 10, including Egyptian, Greek, and Arabic. Wow! That's impressive.

Q Who sent secret messages in food?

A The Ninjas. In the 1500s, these highly trained Japanese assassins and spies sent messages to each other in rice dishes. Each color and pattern in the rice had a secret meaning.

Q Who worshipped turkeys?

A The Mayans. They believed these birds had godlike qualities.

Q Which president spent 27 years in prison?

A Nelson Mandela. He later became the first black president of South Africa. He was a civil rights hero, who helped to create a new country, where black and white people had the same rights and lived side by side.

Q What job did a Roman emperor plan to give his horse?

A Emperor Caligula loved his horse Incitatus so much he wanted to make him a consul, which was a job usually reserved for a human!

Q What were the first toothbrushes made from?

A Pig hair and bamboo. They were made in China in the 1400s. People plucked bristles from hogs or boars and attached them to handles. Very prickly!

Q How did people treat headaches in ancient times?

A One treatment was called "trepanning." It involved drilling a hole into the patient's skull to release whatever was causing the pain.

Q What did the ancient Romans use for mouthwash?

A Their pee! They believed it made their teeth whiter.

Q What on earth did the "Groom of the Stool" do?

A A really horrible job. He helped King Henry VIII of England to wipe his bottom after going to the toilet!

Q Why did a pirate wear an eye patch?

A To help see in the dark. Experts think some pirates wore eye patches to cover missing eyes, while others wore them to help adjust from the bright sunlight on-deck to the darkness below.

Q Which army wore armor made from paper?

A The ancient Chinese. The hardened layers of paper armor could be as strong as metal but there was a problem... it didn't work properly when it got wet.

Q Who worshipped the god of skiing?

A The Vikings. The god Ullr was a skilled skier and hunter. One story says he made the Northern Lights with spray from his skis.

Q In medieval times, how many arrows could an archer fire in a minute?

A About 12.

Q Which was the first country to give women the right to vote?

A New Zealand. It gave women the vote in 1893.

Q Which king made high-heeled shoes fashionable?

A King Louis XIV of France. In the 1670s, he wore shoes with a high red heel.

Q Which American president is rumored to have kept a pet alligator in the White House?

A John Quincy Adams.

Q Which Russian empress hired a herd of cats?

A Empress Elizabeth. In 1745, she was fed up with all the rats and mice in the Winter Palace, so she ordered a load of cats to come and eat them. Around 50 cats still patrol the palace today.

Q What did a thumbs-up sign mean to a gladiator in ancient Rome?

A Nobody knows! It's true that an audience could decide if a gladiator lived or died by using hand and thumb signals. But it's not known which signals meant what.

Q How could a Victorian dress be highly dangerous?

A Its huge skirt could become snagged in a carriage. The fabric could catch fire easily, especially near a fireplace. And some were dyed with arsenic, which is a deadly poison.

Q Which warriors liked to highlight their hair blonde?

A The Vikings. The men washed their hair and beards with a soap full of lye, which is a type of bleach. This powerful soap probably helped to kill head lice, too.

Q Where's New Amsterdam?

A Trick question! New Amsterdam is the old name for New York. In 1664, the British took control of the city, and renamed it New York.

Q How did Khawlah bint al-Azwar rescue her brother?

A This 7th century female Muslim soldier disguised herself as a male knight. She galloped bravely into battle to rescue her brother from a fierce enemy.

Q What do parmesan cheese, seashells, and whale teeth have in common?

A In the past, they were all used as money—the cheese in Italy, the shells across the world, and the teeth in Fiji.

Q What extraordinary weapon may have been used in medieval times in Japan?

A The fart! On an old scroll, there are pictures of a "fart battle," called a He-Gassen. Attackers are seen fleeing from far-reaching gassy farts.

Q When did humans start making art?

A No one knows exactly, but handprints and paintings of animals from 30,000 years ago have been found in caves in France, Australia, and Indonesia.

Q Who had a magnificent wedding feast with 50 delicious courses?

A Catherine de Medici, a powerful Italian princess in the 1400s. Guests ate cold and hot dishes, desserts, and fizzy sherbet drinks. Fancy!

Q How did conkers help the British in WWI?

A Conkers contain acetone, a material used in explosives. British children were encouraged to hand in as many conkers as they could carry in order to help the army make more weapons.

Q What did American president Abraham Lincoln keep in his hat?

A Important state papers to help run the country. What a good way to keep on top of things.

Q Have there ever been baby kings or queens?

A Yep. In 1542, in Scotland, Mary Queen of Scots was just six days old when she was crowned queen. In 1995, in Uganda, three-year-old Oyo became king. At his coronation, he sat on the throne and played with his toys.

Q What did the Aztecs make compulsory?

A School. They took education seriously. Children went to school to learn about the stars and the Aztec way of life.

Q Which body part was left inside an ancient Egyptian mummy?

A The heart. By the way, the brain was removed with a hook through the nose and thrown away!

Q Were there any women pirates?

A Yes! Anne Bonny and Mary Read were fierce pirates on the same ship. And Ching Shih was the most successful pirate of all time! She was known as the "Pirate Queen" and she commanded about 80,000 pirates.

Q Who believed they were descended from dragons?

A Ancient Chinese emperors. Dragons were seen as godlike, wise, and kind.

CUSTOMS + CULTURES

Q How heavy was the largest ever chocolate Easter egg?

A 8 tons—that's heavier than an African bush elephant!

Q When might you throw tomatoes at strangers?

A At the Tomatina festival in Spain. At this massive tomato fight, everyone throws over-ripe really squishy tomatoes at each other for fun. SPLAT!

Q Who worshipped onions?

A The ancient Egyptians. They believed an onion was holy and stood for everlasting life because it was made of many rings.

Q Are Christmas presents only ever given on December 25th?

A In Spain and Mexico, presents are given on "Three Kings Day" on January 6th. In France, presents are opened late at night on December 24th, Christmas Eve.

Q What does a red front door mean?

A In China, a red front door means welcome. In the olden days, in Scotland, a red door meant that the person living inside owned the house.

Q Where in the world is it traditional to slurp noodles on your birthday?

A In China. It's a birthday custom to eat one really long noodle, called a longevity noodle. Long noodles are thought to be lucky for the year ahead. Slurp!

Q When is it ok to eat sweet foods for breakfast?

A At the celebration of Eid-al-Fitr. You might eat sweet creamy pasta with nuts, called sheer korma, or ma'amoul cookies filled with honey. This Muslim festival celebrates the end of a time of fasting, called Ramadan.

Q In which country do school children have classes in knitting?

A Iceland.

Q Who would have smelled sweeter, a Roman soldier or a medieval knight?

A The Roman soldier. Romans liked to stay fresh and clean. They even met at public baths as a social get-together. In medieval times, people washed far less. They thought it was bad for their health. Stinky!

Q Why are there 100 folds in a chef's hat?

A One cooking tradition says that each fold stands for a different way to cook an egg. How many ways can you think of? Fried, boiled...

Q How new is fast food?

A Not new at all! In ancient Roman times, peasants ate at a grab-and-go bar, called a thermopolium.

Q When can you throw paint in the streets?

A In spring, at the Hindu festival of Holi. People sing, dance, and get drenched in colorful paint powder. This festival is based on stories about the god Krishna, who was quite a prankster.

Q Are table manners the same everywhere in the world?

A They change from country to country. In France, it's rude to cut your salad with a knife. In Japan, it's polite to slurp your noodles, and in some countries, burping after a meal is considered a top compliment to the chef.

Q Which sweet treat is a favorite Valentine's Day gift?

A Chocolate. This tradition started in the 1800s.

Q When might you see crowds waving rainbow flags?

A During a Pride Parade, which celebrates the LGBTQ community. There's often dancing, wonderful costumes, and people waving the rainbow flag.

Q Where does the superstition about not walking under a ladder come from?

A Some say from the ancient Egyptians, who thought triangles were a holy shape. The Egyptians believed it was unlucky to walk through a triangle shape made by a ladder leaning against a wall.

Q What brings crowds of people to a hill in Gloucestershire, UK?

A Cheese. Every year, a large wheel of cheese is rolled down Cooper's Hill. Everyone chases after it, hoping to win it for their supper. The race can be pretty dangerous—so don't try it at home!

Q When might a sister give her brother a friendship bracelet?

A During the Hindu festival Raksha Bandhan. A sister ties a bracelet, called a rakhi, around her brother's right wrist, then they agree to look out for each other over the next year.

Q In Roman times, what happened if you broke a mirror?

A It meant seven years of bad luck.

Q What's the difference between a Bar Mitzvah and a Bat Mitzvah?

A A Bar Mitzvah is the ceremony for a Jewish boy becoming a man. And a Bat Mitzvah celebrates a Jewish girl becoming a woman. To wish someone good luck in Hebrew, say "mazel tov."

Q Where do people celebrate New Year with a water fight?

A In Thailand, during the Songkran festival. The idea is to wash away any bad luck from the previous year. Over time, this has turned into massive water fights in the streets.

Q When is it lucky to step in dog poop?

A According to old French myth, it's good luck when you step in it with your left foot. It's bad luck if you step in it with your right.

Q In the past, which spiky fruit made people look posh?

A The pineapple. In the 1800s, wealthy people from European countries loved this fruit because it was so rare. They posed for paintings with pineapples and decorated buildings with pineapple shapes.

Q What was inside the first piñatas?

A Many people believe that the first piñatas were made in ancient China. Paper figures would be filled with seeds, then smashed on to the soil. The Aztecs also had a similar tradition of smashing a clay pot filled with gifts for their god of war. Today, a piñata is filled with candy, then cracked open at a party.

Q What happens if you wear clothes inside out and walk backward on Halloween?

A Legend says you might see a witch at midnight. Common sense says you really won't.

Q Why did the ancient Greeks think garlic breath was a good thing?

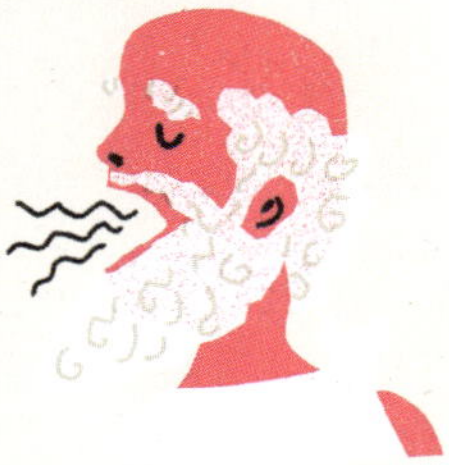

A Because they believed it kept them safe from evil spirits.

Q What happens on the Day of the Dead?

A This Mexican national holiday celebrates loved ones who have died. Families dress up as colorful skeletons, dance, and enjoy delicious food.

Q When is it good to have a big mouth?

A If you're getting married in Russia. The married couple take mouthfuls of wedding cake. The one who takes the bigger bite is seen as head of the family.

Q What is a ceilidh?

A A Scottish gathering where partygoers take part in traditional country dancing. Scottish children often learn the different dances at school.

Q In Russia, when would you say, "Don't hang noodles on my ears!"?

A When you want someone to stop lying to you. Around the world, people have different proverbs, or sayings about life.

Q Where and when would you say "Gesundheit?"

A After someone sneezes. It means "good health" in German. In English, people say "bless you," and in China, a common response is "yi bai sui," which means "may you live a hundred years."

Q What does "Furaha ya kuzaliwa" mean in Swahili?

A Happy Birthday. In Cantorese, you would say, "Sang Yat Fai Lok."

Q Every year in Lopburi, Thailand, there is a huge feast of delicious fruits and vegetables. Who is it for?

A Thousands of macaque monkeys. These monkeys are thought to bring good luck to Lopburi, so every year the people hold the Monkey Buffet Festival to honor their furry friends.

Q What's a moustache cup?

A A special teacup invented in the late 1800s. It was designed to stop the drinker's moustache from getting soggy while they sipped!

Q What day is celebrated on September 19th every year?

A Oo ahhrr, it's Talk Like a Pirate Day. A couple of friends in the USA started the idea of dressing up and talking like pirates all day long. It soon became popular around the world. Ahoy, me hearties.

Q Why do some people think it's unlucky to spill salt?

A Some say it's because in ancient times salt was precious. Roman soldiers were even paid in salt. To spill and waste something so valuable was considered bad luck.

Q Who was the first teacher to assign homework?

A No one knows exactly who to blame for this. But one suspect is the ancient Roman author Pliny, who asked his students to practice speeches at home, before saying them out loud in class.

Q You're in Gujurat, India, on January 14th and you look up at the sky—what do you see?

A Hundreds of kites. Every year on this day, the people of Gujurat fly kites to celebrate the Uttarayan festival, which marks the start of spring in the Hindu calendar.

Q What is the Hajj pilgrimage?

A A religious journey that all Muslims must make at least once in their lifetime, if they can. Every year, around two million Muslims journey from wherever they live to the city of Mecca in Saudi Arabia.

Q What treat do Dutch people eat to celebrate the birth of a baby?

A Mice cookies. Don't worry, no mice are involved in the making of these cookies. The cookies are covered in sugary anise seeds, which look like tiny mice tails.

Q Have we always carved pumpkins at Halloween?

A No. In fact, the tradition started in Ireland, where people carved spooky faces into turnips or potatoes to ward off evil spirits.

Q When might you wear a Venetian mask?

A At the Venice Carnival in Italy. Every year, for hundreds of years, people have dressed in costumes and fancy masks. There are balls, boat parades, and performances to enjoy.

Q What is the haka?

A A group dance performed by Maoris, who are the indigenous people of New Zealand. Originally, the haka was a war dance. Today, hakas are danced at fun occasions, including weddings.

Q What would you find at the Yuki Matsuri festival in Japan?

A Amazing snow and ice sculptures. Millions of visitors admire the towering buildings and figures made from snow and ice.

Q What's the story behind Valentine's day?

A One story is that when the Roman emperor Claudius II banned young people from getting married, a priest called Valentine performed weddings in secret.

Q Boom! Who is the patron saint of fireworks?

A Saint Barbara. A patron saint is a saint from the Catholic Church, who has been chosen to look after a particular group of people or things.

Q What do people all over the world celebrate on April 22nd every year?

A Earth Day. It's a day for people to think about our wonderful planet and share plans or ideas for how to protect it.

Q Is it lucky or unlucky to see a black cat?

A The ancient Egyptians thought all cats were lucky. Many people believe this today. Others think a black cat is a witch in disguise and bad luck.

Q How many days does the Jewish holiday of Hanukkah last for?

A Eight. During Hanukkah, candles are lit on a special candelabra, called a Menorah.

Q Who started the Christmas tree craze?

A The Germans started the tradition in the 1500s. Then in the 1800s, Queen Victoria and her German husband Prince Albert decorated trees with ribbons, candies, and toys. Soon Christmas trees became fashionable all over the world.

OUR WORLD

Q What's the longest place name in the world?

A Taumatawhakatangihangakoauauo-tamateaturipukakapikimaungahoronukup-okaiwhenuakitanatahu. It's the name of a hill in New Zealand and has 85 letters. Phew! Try saying it out loud.

Q What's special about the word "OK?"

A It's one of the most recognizable and frequently used words in the world. Okey dokey!

Q What's the tallest building in the world?

A The Burj Khalifa in Dubai is the current record holder. It's about 2,722 feet tall and has 163 floors. But soon it may be overtaken by Jeddah Tower in Saudi Arabia, which is expected to be 3,280 feet tall.

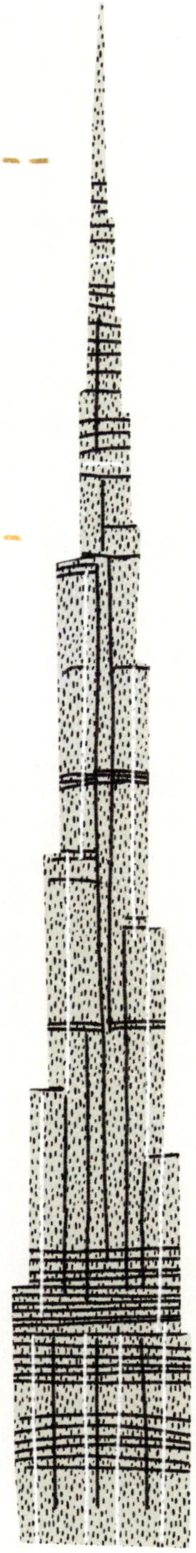

Q Which country has an airport shaped like a dragon?

A China. Beijing's new airport also has triangular windows that look like dragon scales.

Q How many lightbulbs are there at the Sydney Opera House, Australia?

A Every year, around 15,500 light bulbs need to be changed. This vast concert hall is designed to look like the sails of a ship.

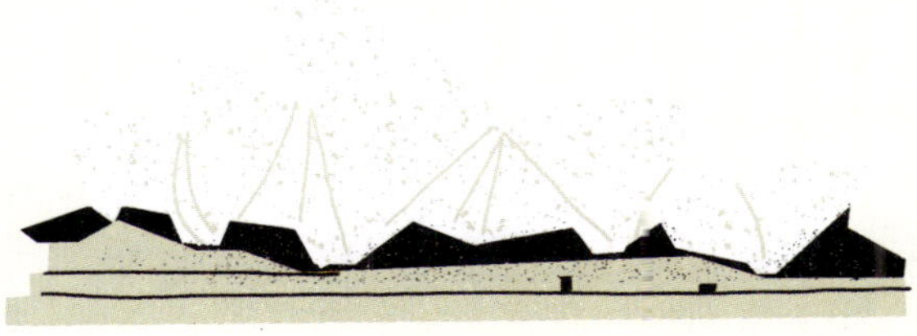

Q Has the Leaning Tower of Pisa EVER been straight?

A Nope. By the time the builders reached the third floor in around 1178, it started leaning. The foundations weren't solid enough in the soft ground.

Q What keeps the bricks in the Great Wall of China stuck together?

A Sticky rice. The wall runs for thousands of miles and is held together with a mixture of sweet rice flour and lime powder.

Q Which colors are used the most in national flags?

A Red, white, and blue. Red is the most popular color of all.

Q How do the Pyramids of Giza in Egypt help tell the time?

A They act like a giant sundial. The ancient Egyptians built the pyramids with such precise measurements, that their shadows show how time passes.

Q How many stars and stripes are on the American flag?

A There are 50 stars, one for each state in the USA. And there are 13 stripes, one for each of the original states.

Q Which are the only three countries to measure in miles, not kilometers?

A USA, Liberia, and Myanmar.

Q Which bridge in Rome, Italy, is haunted?

A Legend has it that if you visit the Ponte Sisto at dawn, you'll see a carriage with a woman inside, speeding out of the city and making off with a stash of stolen gold.

Q How long is the world's longest road?

A About 18,600 miles. It's called the Pan-American Highway and it runs through 14 countries from Alaska to Argentina.

Q What's a cryptocurrency?

A It's a system of tokens, used like money, on the internet. There are no coins or notes. Bitcoin is a famous cryptocurrency.

Q What can you see at the Momofuku Ando Instant Ramen Museum?

A Instant noodles. Oodles and oodles of them! This is a whole museum in Japan dedicated to noodles.

Q What is the Great Pacific Garbage Patch?

A It's a floating mass of garbage in the Pacific Ocean between California and Hawaii, and it's sadly caused by humans. The size of the patch is three times bigger than France.

Q How did the Forbidden City in China get its name?

A For hundreds of years, only the emperor, his family, and those he invited could enter the walls of this vast palace. Today, millions of tourists can visit.

Q Which country has the most people?

A China. Although predictions show that India may soon take over.

Q Which country has more twins than any other?

A Benin, Africa. For every 1,000 births in Benin, about 28 will be twins.

Q Can you name four European countries that start with the letter "S?"

A There are seven to choose from: San Marino, Serbia, Slovakia, Slovenia, Spain, Sweden, and Switzerland.

Q How long is the world's shortest flight?

A Two minutes. That's the official time for this flight between two Scottish islands, but it can be done in just 47 seconds on a good day. Whoosh!

Q How many languages are spoken in the world?

A Almost 7,000.

Q What does the red circle in the Japanese flag stand for?

A The Sun. Japan is sometimes called the Land of the Rising Sun.

Q Why is the Golden Gate Bridge in San Francisco, orange?

A The plan was to paint it blue and yellow, but the primer, or first coat, was orange. Everyone liked the orange so much, it stuck.

Q What is the Statue of Liberty's torch made of?

A Copper, mostly. But the outside is covered in gold leaf, which is gold that has been hammered into a very thin sheet.

Q How many people live in the world?

A Almost 8 billion. By the year 2050, there might be nearly 10 billion people in the world. That's a lot of people.

Q What's the smallest country in the world?

A Vatican City. It's governed by the Catholic Church. Fewer than 1,000 people live there.

Q Which country has the longest national anthem in world?

A Greece. It's got 158 verses.

Q Which two countries have almost identical orange, green, and white flags?

A Ireland and the Ivory Coast. This really is a double take!

Q What is Scotland's national animal?

A The unicorn.

Q What would you find on Easter Island?

A Almost 1,000 giant statues known as moai. They were carved by humans about 500 years ago.

Q What can you NOT wear inside the British Houses of Parliament?

A A law dating back to the 1300s forbids a person from wearing a suit of armor. This law still exists today.

Q Who cycled down the Eiffel Tower in Paris?

A In 1923, a journalist called Pierre Labric cycled down the steps from the first floor. Must have been a bumpy ride!

Q How many elephants helped build the Taj Mahal in India?

A Over 1,000 elephants helped carry vast marble blocks to build this huge mausoleum, or tomb. Emperor Shah Jahan had it built for his wife, Mumtaz Mahal, who had died.

Q Which is the biggest country in the world?

A Russia. It's huge. It's bigger than the surface area of the dwarf planet Pluto.

Q How was Stonehenge built?

A We don't know! It's still a mystery how ancient people built this stone circle in England. Each of the bigger stones weighs as much as four African bush elephants.

Q Which continent has no countries?

A Antarctica.

Q Which country serves up the hamburger as its national dish?

A The USA.

Q What can you find beneath the streets of Paris, France?

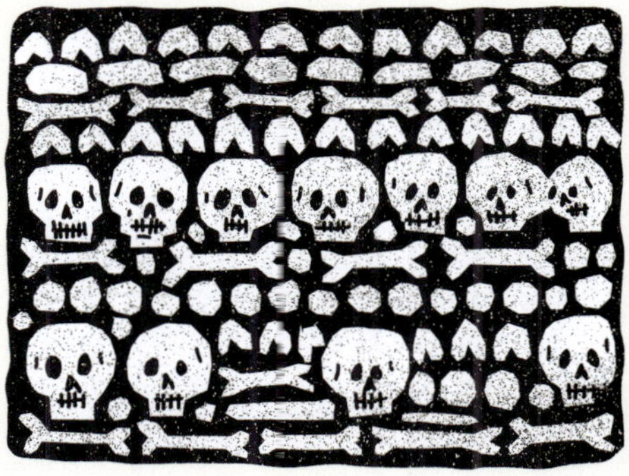

A Miles of spooky tunnels called catacombs that house the skeletons of over 6 million people! They were placed there hundreds of years ago when cemeteries above ground ran out of room.

Q Have snowball fights ever been banned?

A Yes. Up until 2019, a town in Colorado had an old law banning people from throwing snowballs. A nine-year-old boy challenged the law in 2019 and now people are free to fling.

Q Which country's national motto is "Harambee," and what does it mean?

A Kenya. It means "All pull together."

Q Which is the longest train journey in the world?

A The Trans-Siberian Express, which runs across Russia. It starts in Moscow and travels across Siberia to Vladivostok. The journey takes six days.

Q Which language is spoken by the most people in the world?

A Mandarin Chinese.

Q Which fancy metro station has chandeliers?

A The Komsomolskaya station, in Moscow, Russia. Travelers look up to see chandeliers hanging from decorated yellow ceilings, just like a ballroom.

Q Does "Ciao" mean hello or goodbye in Italian?

A Trick question. It can mean both. And in Hawaii, "Aloha" means hello and goodbye, too.

Q Which country hosts the mud Olympics every year?

A Germany. Events include muddy soccer and muddy volleyball.

Q India, Vietnam, and Egypt all share the same national flower—what is it?

A It's the lotus flower. These flowers are seen as symbols of purity and rebirth. Their roots grow in murky waters while their beautiful flowers rest on the surface.

Q Which towering city wall was smashed down in 1989?

A The Berlin Wall in Germany. It had kept the east and west sides of the city separated for nearly 30 years.

Q Which city is thought to have more bicycles than people?

A Amsterdam in the Netherlands.

Q Which ancient Roman amphitheater was also a boating lake?

A The Colosseum in Rome, Italy. One day, gladiators fought each other in a sandy arena. The next day, the building could be flooded for a mock sea battle with model ships.

ARTS + ENTERTAINMENT

Q How many ways can you shuffle a pack of playing cards?

A Mathematicians say around 80,000,000,000,000,000,000,000, 000,000,000,000,000,000,000, 000,000,000,000,000,000,000,000 ways. That's "8" followed 67 zeros! It's very unlikely the 52 cards will ever shuffle the same way twice.

Q What's Welly Wanging?

A It's a sport. Contestants throw Wellington boots as far as they can. Some hurl the boots backward over their heads!

Q Which French-American artist exhibited a urinal in an art gallery?

A Marcel Duchamp. In 1917, he entered an art competition with a porcelain urinal, called "Fountain." He often made people think about what makes something art.

Q How many people watch the Summer Olympics on TV?

A Around 3 billion.

Q How many people danced in the world's biggest "chicken dance?"

A In 1996, at a county fair in the USA, wait for it, 72,000 people flapped their arms like wings to "The Chicken Song"—a song often played at sports events.

Q What is Cuju?

A An ancient Chinese sport similar to soccer. Just imagine, a type of soccer was first played over 2,000 years ago!

Q Which poem takes eight hours to read out loud?

A The *Mahabharata*, an ancient Indian epic poem that's about 1.8 million words long. It tells the story of battling royal families.

Q In which American city was jazz music first played?

A New Orleans.

Q What does the word "supercalifragilistic-expialidocious" mean?

A Wonderful and really very good. It was made popular in the first Mary Poppins movie. Next time you feel wonderful, try saying it out loud.

Q Which cat helped write classical music?

A A pet cat named Pulcinella. The 18th century Italian composer Domenico Scarlatti wrote a musical piece called the "cat fugue," inspired by Pulcinella walking across the keys of his piano.

Q Who invented chess?

A Many believe the game chess is based on an ancient Indian game, called Chaturanga, where there are elephants and chariots, instead of bishops and rooks.

Q Which painting was accidentally hung upside down in an art gallery?

A French artist Henri Matisse's picture *Le Bateau*, was hung upside down in New York's Museum of Modern Art for two months, until a visitor eventually noticed.

Q What special effects did William Shakespeare use during performances of his plays?

A Smoke, trapdoors, fire, actors lifted into the air on wires—he even used cannons!

Q Can music ever be silent?

A In 1952, the American composer John Cage created a song of four minutes and 33 seconds of silence. There are no sounds at all.

Q Which famous Dutch artist painted pictures of sunflowers and died penniless?

A Vincent van Gogh. He had an unhappy life and sold only one painting in his lifetime. Today, his paintings sell for millions.

Q What are comic books called in Japan?

A Manga. When you read a manga magazine in Japanese, you read the words from right to left.

Q When were fireworks invented?

A Around 2,000 years ago, ir China. Do you think the spectators 'Ooched' and 'Aaahed' like we do today?

Q Has the Incredible Hulk always been green?

A When he first appeared in a comic, he was gray. It was difficult to print the color gray so the Hulk became green.

Q How much TV does a child watch every year?

A Well, if a child watches about two hours of TV every day for a year, it adds up to around 730 hours. That's about the same as one whole month!

Q How old was the Austrian composer Mozart when he first performed?

A Just five years old.

Q What did the first tennis players use to hit the ball?

A The palms of their hands! Game, set, match.

Q How small is the smallest book in the world?

A Too small to see with your eyes! It measures 70 micrometers x 100 micrometers, which is about as thick as a hair on your head.

Q What's Pong?

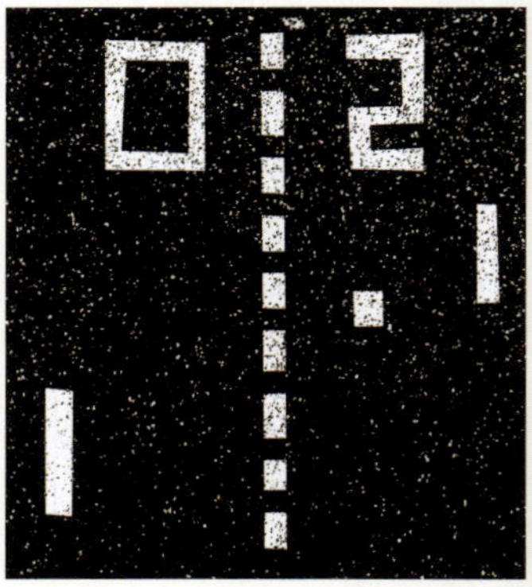

A One of the first video games. Invented in 1972, it was based on table tennis and became very popular.

Q What's made in Nollywood, Bollywood, and Hollywood?

A Movies. Nollywood is in Nigeria, Bollywood is in India, and Hollywood is in the USA.

Q What's B-612?

A It's the asteroid that's home to the prince in the story *The Little Prince* by French writer Antoine de Saint-Exupéry.

Q What did a jester do in medieval times?

A A jester's job was to entertain. They wore bright clothes, danced, juggled, told stories, and did magic tricks.

Q Can a child write a bestselling novel?

A Definitely. In 1890, a nine-year-old British girl called Daisy Ashford wrote *The Young Visiters*, then forgot about it. Twenty-nine years later, it was published and became a big success. Keep on writing!

Q How are dinosaur sounds made in the movies?

A Nobody knows what dinosaurs sounded like, so movie makers guess and use all sorts of noises, including recordings of trumpeting baby elephants.

Q Which spooky story was originally called The Dead Un-dead?

A *Dracula*, by Irish author Bram Stoker. The evil vampire Dracula sucks blood from his victims and changes shape into a bat.

Q What happens when you listen to music?

A Scientists say music can improve your mood, memory, concentration, and sleep.

Q How old is the oldest working Ferris wheel in the world?

A Over 100 years old! It was built in 1897 in Austria and is still operating today.

Q What does "karaoke" mean?

A This Japanese word means "empty orchestra." Karaoke is a games machine that lets you sing along to your favorite songs.

Q What's one of the oldest musical instruments?

A The didgeridoo. It makes a deep 'ooo' sound. In Australia, this instrument has been played for thousands of years. It's traditionally made from a tree trunk hollowed out by termites.

Q What did the first ballet dancers have in common?

A They were all men! When ballet was first introduced, women were banned from dancing.

Q Which Mexican artist had two pet monkeys?

A Frida Kahlo. The monkeys were called Fulang Chang and Caimito de Guayabal. She had a parrot called Bonito, too.

Q How far and fast does your TV signal travel?

A Satellites high up in space send and receive radio signals to show pictures on your TV. These signals travel about 23,600 miles in about 0.13 seconds. That's about as fast as the blink of an eye!

Q Which famous painting has its own mailbox?

A The *Mona Lisa* by Italian artist Leonardo da Vinci. People love this painting of a smiling woman so much, they send it love letters.

Q What did the ancient Greeks do at the end of a play?

A Stomp their feet. Then, over the years, people clapped their hands instead. The ancient Greeks also booed and made donkey noises when they didn't like something.

Q What is Donald Duck's middle name?

A Fauntleroy.

Q How many pieces of wood do you need to make a violin?

A About 70.

Q What inspired Roald Dahl to write Charlie and the Chocolate Factory?

A Rumor has it he was partly inspired by his experience as a taster for Cadbury chocolate bars as a boy.

Q Can a computer beat a human at chess?

A Yes. In 1997, a computer called Deep Blue beat the Russian chess champion Gary Kasparov.

Q How long has the yo-yo been spinning?

A About 2,500 years! Rumor has it that the ancient Greeks invented the first yo-yos, made from terracotta clay.

Q Why is everyone so serious in old black and white photographs?

A In the 1800s, it took hours for a photographer to take a single photo. People sat as still as they could for a very long time, but it was too long to keep smiling.

Q Which story starts, "All children, except one, grow up."?

A *Peter Pan* by Scottish writer J.M. Barrie. Peter has a never-ending childhood in a land called Neverland.

Q How long is the world's longest rollercoaster?

A Almost 1.5 miles long. It's called the Steel Dragon 2000 and it's in Japan. It takes four minutes to ride it.

Q What's the highest score you can get in ten-pin bowling?

A 300. You'd have to bowl 12 perfect strikes to reach it.

Q What would you find at an "anatomical theater?"

A A gruesome sight. Anatomical means to study the body. And in the 1500s, people paid to watch corpses, or dead bodies, being dissected. Yuck!

Q How did the trampoline bounce into action?

A One day in the 1930s, 16-year-old American George Nissen saw circus performers on a high wire and thought it looked fun to drop on to the safety net below, so he invented the trampoline. BOING!

Q The "box," "flat," and "sled" are what kind of toy?

A Kites.

JARGON BUSTER

A

antennae

Feelers on the head of insects and some other animals, which are used to sense their surroundings.

artery

A thick tube that carries blood from the heart all the way around the body. Arteries carry blood 24 hours a day, every day.

astronomer

An astronomer studies the wonders of space, including the Sun, moon, planets, and stars.

atmosphere

The blanket of gases that surrounds Earth. It helps to keep our planet the correct temperature, not too hot or too cold.

atom

A basic unit of matter. Everything in the universe is made from atoms.

B

bacteria

Minute living things, each made from just one cell. Some are good and some are harmful. You need a microscope to see bacteria.

biofuel

A type of fuel made from living matter, such as plants and even animal poop.

black hole

A black hole is a super-strong force in space that swallows up everything nearby.

blood vessel

Tubes that carry blood around a body. Arteries and veins are types of blood vessels.

C

cell

All living things are made from cells. The cell is the smallest unit of life. An amoeba is made from one cell. A human being is made from trillions of cells.

civil rights

The rights, or freedoms, that make sure you and everyone else gets treated fairly, whatever your gender, religion, or the color of your skin, or if you have a disability.

climate change

Climate is the pattern of weather around the world over a long period of time. Scientists say that the climate is changing because the world is becoming hotter.

clockwise and counterclockwise

Think of the hands on a clock. Clockwise is the direction of a clock going forward. Counterclockwise is the direction of a clock going backward.

clone

When you clone something, you make an identical copy in every way.

continent

A huge mass of land. There are seven continents on Earth—Asia, Africa, North America, South America, Antarctica, Europe, and Australia.

D

data

All the unbelievable facts in this book are data that have been gathered together. Data is a collection of information, especially facts or numbers.

E

empire

A group of lands and people ruled by just one leader, an emperor or an empress. The Roman empire stretched for thousands of miles.

epic poem

A long poem that tells a dramatic story full of heroes, heroines, and adventure.

equator

An imaginary line that goes all the way around the middle of the Earth. Places near the equator are called tropical.

F

fossil

The remains of living things preserved in rocks. Fossils may be thousands or millions of years old. We know about dinosaurs because of dinosaur fossils.

G

galaxy

A huge collection of planets, dust, gas, and billions of stars. Earth is in the galaxy called the Milky Way.

gas

The air we breathe is made from gases. Gas has no fixed shape or size, so it moves and flows freely.

germ

A living thing made from one cell. It's also called a bacterium. When germs get into your body, they make you sick.

gravity

A powerful invisible force that pulls everything downward. On Earth, gravity helps to keep our feet on the ground.

H

hemisphere

The top half of the world is called the Northern Hemisphere. The bottom half of the world is called the Southern Hemisphere.

hormone

A chemical inside plants and animals, including humans, that passes on messages to do particular things. For example, when you are scared or excited, hormones give you energy.

I

ice age

A period of very cold climate around the world, with large areas of land covered by glaciers and thick sheets of ice. Big ice ages may last for hundreds of millions of years.

indigenous people

The group of people who lived in a place first. Maoris lived in New Zealand long before settlers arrived in the 1900s.

intestine

The part of your body that helps you to take in the nutrients, or goodness, from food. There is a big and a small intestine.

ISS

ISS stands for International Space Station, which is a large spacecraft that orbits Earth. On board, astronauts from many countries do science experiments.

L

lava

When a volcano blows its top, hot liquid rock, called lava, spews out. When the lava cools, it hardens to rock.

LGBTQ

These letters stand for lesbian, gay, bisexual, trans, and queer. LGBTQ celebrates the many different ways that people live and have families together.

M

matter

This is all the stuff around you, including your body, the air you breathe, and this book. Matter is made from lots of atoms.

medieval

A time in history from about the year 500 to 1500. In medieval times, in Europe, there were knights and castles.

meteoroid

A small chunk of rock that zips through space. If the rock enters Earth's atmosphere, it burns up and you might see it as a meteor, or shooting star.

N

nerve

Nerves carry signals around a body and help it to sense and respond to its surroundings. You have nerve endings on your fingertips.

O

orbit

To orbit means to travel around something. The Earth orbits the Sun.

oxygen

Air contains oxygen, which is a gas that you can't see or smell. Living things need oxygen to survive.

P

pharaoh

In ancient Egypt, a pharaoh belonged to a royal family and ruled with absolute power.

phobia

A phobia is when someone has a terror of something, such as flying.

plague

When a deadly and very infectious disease spreads quickly from one person to another, it's called a plague.

protein

Protein helps the body to grow. Protein is found in meat, milk, eggs, and beans.

R

Ring of Fire

An area around the Pacific Ocean. Here, plates that make up the Earth's surface are uneven and overlap, so there are many volcanoes and earthquakes.

S

solar system

Our group of planets, including Earth, that orbits the Sun. In space, there are other solar systems, too.

species

A group of living things which have particular characteristics in common. Humans are a species; so are giant pandas and emperor penguins.

V

vaccine

Usually a vaccine is an injection. It stops you from catching a disease by giving you a small dose of a dead or weak form of the disease. It makes your body build up a resistance.

vein

In the body, this thin tube carries blood back to the heart. You have a network of veins.

W

water cycle

The everlasting journey of water around our world, from the rain that falls from the clouds on to the land, oceans, and lakes, to the watery mist that rises up again to form clouds in the sky.

INDEX

For Seth and Joe. – J. W.

For Frankie. – L. L.

Brimming with creative inspiration, how-to projects, and useful information to enrich your everyday life, Quarto Knows is a favourite destination for those pursuing their interests and passions. Visit our site and dig deeper with our books into your area of interest: Quarto Creates, Quarto Cooks, Quarto Homes, Quarto Lives, Quarto Drives, Quarto Explores, Quarto Gifts, or Quarto Kids.

This edition published in 2021 by Chartwell Books,
an imprint of The Quarto Group
142 West 36th Street, 4th Floor
New York, NY 10018 USA
T (212) 779-4972 F (212) 779-6058
www.QuartoKnows.com

First published in 2021 by Frances Lincoln Children's Books,
an imprint of The Quarto Group.
The Old Brewery, 6 Blundell Street, London N7 9BH, United Kingdom.
T (0)20 7700 6700 F (0)20 7700 8066 www.QuartoKnows.com

10 9 8 7 6 5 4 3 2 1

Chartwell titles are also available at discount for retail, wholesale, promotional, and bulk purchase. For details, contact the Special Sales Manager by email at specialsales@quarto.com or by mail at The Quarto Group, Attn: Special Sales Manager, 100 Cummings Center Suite 265D, Beverly, MA 01915, USA.

ISBN: 978-0-7858-4063-3

Published by Katie Cotton
Designed by Sasha Moxon
Cover Designed by Kate Sinclair
Edited by Hannah Dove
Production by Dawn Cameron
Fact-checked by Dr Barbara Taylor and Robin Pridy

Printed in China

FSC
www.fsc.org
MIX
Paper from responsible sources
FSC® C016973